D1616289

# Pipe

# Pipe

## The Art and Lore of a Great Tradition

Robin Crole

PRIMA PUBLISHING

Pipe: The Art & Lore of a Great Tradition
© 1999 by Prima Editions

PRIMA PUBLISHING and colophon are registered trademarks of Prima Communications, Inc.

Library of Congress Cataloging-in-Publication Data

Crole, Robin.
    Pipe : the art and lore of a great tradition / Robin Crole.
       p.   cm.
    Includes bibliographical references and index.
    ISBN 0-7615-1507-0
    1. Tobacco pipes. 2. Smoking—History. I. Title.
GT3020 .C73    1999
394.1'4—dc21                       99-32960
                                    CIP

Illustrations by Oliver Frey
Cover photograph by Steven Paul Associates
Production: Matthew Uffindell
Design and four-color separation by Prima Creative Services, England
Printed and bound in Italy by Rotolito Lombarda

## Picture Credits:

The Advertising Archives: 49, 49, 49, 55, 138; AKG Photo: 34, 42, 44, 45, 47, 48, 56, 58, 58, 59, 62, 74, 135; Ann Ronan-Image Select International: 21, 29, 30, 32, 38, 39, 42, 63, 66, 71, 77, 77, 79, 91, 115; Bridgeman: 11, 18, 26, 27, 37, 38, 39, 41; Bridgeman-Giraudon: 22, 28, 35, 35, 36, 136; E.T. Archive: 6, 14, 44, 45, 47, 53, 59, 60, 63, 75, 78, 82; The Fotomax Index: 16, 20; G.S.F. Picture Library: 81; Gawith-Hoggarth, Kendal: 122; Giraudon: 31, 34, 139; Giraudon Arras Musée des Beaux Arts: 43; Hulton Getty: 48, 54, 55, 56, 61, 64, 87; Hulton Getty-FPG: 46, 56, 71, 76, 80, 80, 86, 88, 124; Image Bank: 85, 121, 125, 134; Image Select International: 21, 40, 66, 67, 118, 137; J. Allan Cash Ltd: 66, 84, 92, 119, 120, 120, 137; Keystone: 52; Kobal Collection: 68, 68, 69, 69, 69, 110; Lauros-Giraudon: 27, 33, 65, 72; Mary Evans: 12, 13, 15, 17, 23, 29, 30, 38, 40, 41, 50, 51, 53, 57, 58; McGahey Ltd: 132; Peterson of Dublin: 96, 96, 96, 97, 98, 98, 98, 98, 98, 98, 100; Planet Earth Pictures: 83, 96, 117, 118, 119; Prima Editions: 139; Robin Crole: 93; Spectrum Color Library: 70, 89, 90, 138; Steven Paul Associates-Prima Editions: 2, 5, 6, 94, 99, 99, 103, 104, 105, 106, 107, 109, 111, 113, 123, 126, 127, 128, 129, 131, 132, 133; Superstock: 16, 68, 114, 116, 117; Superstock-Newberry Library, Chicago: 73; Vauen, Germany: 108; Illustrations by Oliver Frey & Prima Editions: 10, 13, 14, 14, 24, 25, 74, 75, 76, 82, 88, 91, 93, 97, 100, 101, 102, 129, 130, 131, 140.

## Acknowledgments:

The publishers and the author gratefully acknowledge the assistance and information from:
Alan Myerthall, The Pipe Shop, Leith Walk, Edinburgh; the discriminating smokers, Michael Campbell and Paul Ledger; the companies, Petersons of Dublin, Gawith Hoggarth Ltd & Co and Samuel Gawith & Co of Kendal, Peretti of Boston, Courrieu of Cogolin; Tobacco Merchants Association, (U.S.A.), Tobacco Manufacturers Association, (U.K.); the U.S. Embassy Information Service, London; the Health Education Board of Scotland; the Pipe Smoker's Council, (U.K.), and especially to Martin McGahey the Tobacconist, Exeter, England, for kindly supplying the pipes and pipe smoking materials used in many of the photographs in this book, as well as much invaluable advice. You can reach McGahey on the internet at: **www.the-tobacconist.co.uk**

### How to Order

Single copies may be ordered from Prima Publishing, P.O. Box 1260BK, Rocklin, CA 95677; telephone (916) 632-4400. Quantity discounts are also available. On your letterhead, include information concerning the intended use of the books and the number of books you wish to purchase.

Visit us online at www.primalifestyles.com

*Page 2:* **Classic Italian from Savinelli.**

*Opposite:* **The beautiful sheen of a pure jade bowl from the firm of Comoy.**

*Page 6:* **A fine example of elegance from Butz-Choquin, one of the largest factories in Saint-Claude, France.**

# Pipe

# Table of Contents

Pipe

# Introduction

Apipe jutting forcefully from a clenched mouth is an arche-typal image. It is as if this thin stem with its bowl from which wafts aromatic smoke has been with us forever.

A man and his pipe.

There is no need to explain a person beyond this image. Determined, yet calm, relaxed, yet focused—the pipe smoker is a character of his own. A civilized person, coping with any situation, whether charged with action or steeped in profound thought—or relaxed in a way that modern life sometimes seems to render impossible.

And yet it is these modern days that are witnessing a rejuvenation of the image of the pipe smoker. Young people are rediscovering the habit and deeming it cool.

Can pipe smoking be fashionable again?

The truth is that it was the height of fashion hundreds of years ago, when it was a new-fangled activity, when the equivalent of today's cool youth would not be seen without a pipe.

Today, young new aficionados stake their claim to join the circle of the brotherhood. It is not age that counts, it is the special appreciation of a pleasurable ritual of calm in a proverbial storm which links young and old in the shared enjoyment of a newly appreciated puff of the pipe smoke.

If pipe smokers are a minority, what a very select group of people they are. This book celebrates them, past and present—and most of all, it celebrates what makes them what they are: the pipes and the tobacco in all their fine array.

# Pipe

*"Tobacco, divine, rare, superexcellent."*

"Anatomy of Melancholy," Robert Burton, 1621

CHAPTER ONE

# The Magic of Smoke

Robert Burton (1577–1640), quoted above, was an English writer and clergyman. His *Anatomy of Melancholy* is described by Chambers Bibliographical Dictionary (1990) as "a vast and witty compendium of Jacobean knowledge about the 'disease' of melancholy..."

Beside the rippling river, a triumphant fisherman lays his trout upon a frond of fern. Warm in the spring sunshine, he rests his rod against the bank and fills his pipe. Cupping his hands around the bowl against the wind, he coaxes the tobacco to smolder and lies back on his elbow in an ecstasy of pleasure. The trout as he eyes it seems to grow larger; the smoke as he watches it drives away the midges and leads him to the pipe dreams of the past.

While smoke has, from the very earliest times, been associated with superstition and religion, our fisherman's roving thoughts would find no mention of the actual habit of smoking in the Bible or Shakespeare; nor did the Greeks or Romans have a word for it—unlike later armies, the legionaries of the empire marched without its solace.

The Greek historian, Herodotus (c.485–425 BC), is usually credited with the first mention of smoking, when he described the habit of the wild Scythian horsemen escaping the harsh realities of the steppe life. He noted that they threw leaves of an unknown plant on the fire and sat around inhaling the smoke.

Herodotus: the first reporter on the habit of smoking.

# ᴘ̲ipe̲

The Delphic Oracle of ancient Greece, set on the flanks of Mount Parnassus, was one of many such religious places where ordinary men and women could ask the gods for advice on how they should act in moments of personal crisis. The smoke of burned aromatic herbs no doubt added to the awe and fear which the Pythian priestess of Apollo instilled in her supplicants as she relayed the gods' wisdom.

"They grow drunk with the fumes, as the Greeks do with wine," he wrote, "until they jump up and begin to dance and sing."

This plant was almost certainly hemp, or *Cannabis sativa*, now widely known by the names of its derivatives: marijuana, hashish, charas, ghanja, bhang, kef, and dagga. Tobacco itself was not known to the world outside the as yet undiscovered Americas, and it would not be for centuries.

However, a large variety of aromatic herbs were burned to enhance religious ceremonies—and even induce hallucinations—throughout the world. It is quite probable, for example, that the Pythian priestess at the Delphic Oracle on Parnassus secretly fed leaves to the hot vapors arising from the cleft in the mountain to intoxicate both herself and her anxious customers before pronouncing words of divine purpose. Certainly it would seem that when the priests led visitors, such as the hero Odysseus, to the House of the Dead on the Acheron River, the legendary Styx of Hades, they lowered them down on a primitive lift into a fume-laden chamber to confuse and awe them. Remnants of this contraption can be viewed in the museum at Ioannina.

This ceremonial use of scented, and often mind-expanding, smoke continued right into medieval times, without ever being thought of as a source of everyday pleasure. Inspiration for this would come from a continent awaiting discovery.

**Columbus makes peace offerings to the natives. In return they gave him the peace pipe.**

### Fateful Journey

In 1492, as every schoolchild knows, Columbus crossed the ocean blue to reach the fabled Indies, only to hit upon the Americas. That year was to be when the world at large first discovered tobacco—and tobacco smoking.

Although new and strange to the European explorers, the cultivation of the plant and the habit of smoking had been widespread in the Americas for a long time. In fact, the oldest pipes so far were discovered in the so-called pipe mounds of the Mississippi basin. Attributed to the Hopewell culture that arose around 300 B.C., the finds are such beautifully carved bowls of animal and human form that they can only have been used for ritual, in a manner foreshadowing the pipe's later importance to the North American Indians. Farther south, Central America shows evidence of having been the center from which the general practice of smoking spread. At the time of the birth of Christ, the Mayan god Chak, as shown in a bas relief stone sculpture to be found in the ruined city of Palenque in Mexico, was feting his worshippers with pipe smoke.

**This pipe with a heron totem is typical of the so-called "mound pipes" found in the Mississippi basin.**

# Pipe

Nearby, dating from the second century A.D., can be seen a carving of a priest wearing a jaguar skin cloak and a headdress representing a mythical bird, who is blowing out a smoke offering through a straight tube.

There are traditions outside the Americas of crude smoking, in these cases of hemp. In Africa the Bushmen of the Kalahari had a primitive practice of earth smoking, which may have been widespread throughout the continent. First they ignited herbs in an earthen hearth. Through the clay rim of this giant bowl, they then inserted hollow reeds so that, lying down, they could inhale the fumes of the drug.

This does not compare with the sophistication discovered in the New World. Clay pipes dug up in widely scattered areas are ample evidence of pre-Columbian smoking in Central and North America. Samples found in Mexico are elaborately molded and ornamented as if they had a ritual as well as a social use. Elsewhere both divine Chak and ordinary mortals are shown with their tube pipes, suggesting a long-established practice.

From Mexico the habit must have spread to the Indians of North America. There, like nowhere else in the world until modern times, tobacco assumed a wholly integrated part in the daily round of life and its ritual. We know it best from the peace pipe or calumet, smoked on ceremonial occasions—where curiously the stem was more important than the bowl—but in different forms and usages smoking was practiced among most of the North American tribes. The plains Indians would appoint the possessor of a pipe of known spiritual power to lead their war parties. Among the Indians of the Southwest, the village chief was known as the Keeper of the Sacred Smoke. It is told of the Natchez tribes, the inheritors of the Hopewell culture without their artistic skills, that on the death of their paramount leader, the Great Sun (the ordinary members of his tribe were called Stinkers), his wives and retinue were ceremonially anesthetized with tobacco and strangled.

The tobacco used by the North American Indians was cultivated and collected from the wild and sometimes mixed with other substances such as willow bark, which they called *kinikinik*. This was presumably the nasty con-

A stone bas-relief found in Palenque, Mexico shows a Mayan priest smoking a tube pipe, while below a Maya man sits to enjoy a quiet puff.

Pottery figurine showing a person smoking a pipe, from the Tachina culture of Ecuardor, c. 500 BC.

coction that was used to subdue the Stinkers.

By the time Columbus reached the Indies, the habit of pipe smoking prevailed among almost all the Indian tribes of North, Central, and South America.

The contemplative pipe smoker might well wonder how the ingrained habits of Indian tribes in a then remote and isolated part of the world came to spread and grow into such a powerful and universal social preoccupation, if not need.

## Birth of a Habit

While the rest of the world smoked (if they smoked at all) hemp, the fumes that Columbus and his shipmates encountered in Cuba came from *Nicotiana tabacum*, which is the parent of the plant used for the most part today, and the natives of Virginia, from whom the British were to learn the art, smoked a wild tobacco, *Nicotiana rusticana*.

Columbus reported that for ceremonial smoking in the Antilles a Y-shaped tube was used. Its horns were inserted into the nostrils to induce, by inhalation of smoke, a state of trance. Las Casas, chronicler of Columbus's first voyage, wrote that the

This fanciful engraving of c.1600 depicts a native North American savoring the tobacco that has been prepared by his fellow tribesmen in the background.

# Pipe

Indians had "a firebrand in their hands and certain herbs for smoking. These were dry and placed in a dry leaf after the manner of those paper tubes which boys in Spain use at Whitsuntide."

Columbus himself described the practice, writing in his diary November 6, 1493, from Cuba:

*"My two messengers reported that they had encountered many men and women carrying some sort of cylinder in which sweet smelling herbs were glowing. These they supposed were dried leaf stalks covered by equally dry but broader leaf. The people sucked the other ends and, as it were, drank in the smoke. Although this apparently intoxicated them, it also seemed to protect them from fatigue. The natives said that they called these cylinders 'tabacos.'"*

Hemp was the commonest leaf smoked until the spread of tobacco from Cuba.

American natives gathering hemp and enjoying the effects of their labors.

16

A few years later Cortez and his men at the court of Montezuma were offered drinking chocolate for breakfast, together with a dried golden leaf to be "drunk" from golden tubes.

Thus, the reports of this wonder reached Europe, and in 1568 Francisco Fernandez was sent by Philip II of Spain to investigate the products of Mexico. He returned bearing the tobacco plant, and soon Jean Nicot, French ambassador to Portugal, obtained some of its seeds and sent them to his queen, thus unwittingly ensuring his place in the common language by lending his name to the genus *Nicotiana* and the alkaloid nicotine.

Nicot was primarily interested in tobacco's medical properties, and the plant arrived in continental Europe essentially as a medicament and a garden flower. In England, however, tobacco was seized upon for its smoke. In Othello, Shakespeare has Iago refer to the English in their drinking habits as most potent in "potting." We might say that if the bard's mythical meeting with the adventurer Sir Walter Raleigh had ever taken place, he might have added, "And potent at piping." Elizabethan England became obsessed by pipe smoking, and even the queen had a shot at it. A doggerel runs that pipe smokers should:

Jean Nicot,
the man who gave
us nicotine.

> *"The debt confess though nonetheless*
> *They love the grape and barley,*
> *Which Frenchmen owe to Jean Nicot*
> *And Englishmen to Raleigh."*

Sir Walter is sometimes mistakenly credited with the introduction of tobacco into England. He appointed Ralph Lane to be governor of the first settlement in Virginia but never went there himself. When Lane returned one disastrous year later in 1586, he and his men had certainly learned the use of the plant from their contact with the East Coast tribes. But it was the earlier seamen returning from

their dramatic voyages of exploration who brought back both the seed and the habit.

Nicot, too, seems to have been anticipated. In 1525 a Dieppe mapmaker, Pierre Grignon, wrote:

> "Yesterday I met an old sailor with whom I took a glass of Breton wine. While drinking he suddenly brought out of his bag a white object which I thought at first to be a school-boy's writing instrument—one would have said an inkwell with a long pipe attached—and a small wallet. He filled the large end with some brown leaves which he had crushed in the hollow of his hand, applied fire to it by an ember, and a moment later, having put the pipe between his lips, he puffed out the smoke from his mouth which astonished me. He told me that the Portuguese had taught him and that they had learnt it from the Mexican Indians. He called it 'petuner,' and said that it inspired him and gave him pleas-ant thoughts."

Forty years later, John Sparke sailed with Sir John Hawkins to the Indies and Florida, and he described the taking of tobacco:

> "The Florideans have a kinde of herbe dried, who with a cane and earthen cup in the end, with fire and the dried herbs put together, doe sucke throw the cane the smoke thereof which satisfieth their hunger and therewith they have four or five days without meate and drinke, and this all Frenchmen use for the purpose."

**Sir Walter Raleigh's first smoke must have been a revelation, at least as portrayed in this whimsical Victorian painting. Almost by definition, the dog is England's first passive smoker.**

From across the Atlantic through the ports of southwest England, the seamen's habit spread inland. Two doctors, in a Latin account dedicated to Queen Elizabeth, wrote in 1570:

> "You may see sailors and all those who come back from America, carrying little funnels, pusilla infundibula, made from a palm leaf or a reed, in the extreme end of which they insert the rolled and powdered dried leaves of this plant."

Three years later another writer recorded that the taking of "smoke by an instrument loke a little ladle is gretlie taken up in England."

By the turn of the century, the plant, which is tolerant of different climatic conditions, was growing happily in England and, together with Virginian imports or seizures from the Spanish galleons, was in high demand. The pipe made of clay had become established as the most satisfactory instrument, and the actual word pipe was first mentioned in a dictionary as early as 1596. Alehouses became tobacco clubs where, when the price of tobacco was too high, the pipe was shared around among the company. Walter Raleigh, Queen Elizabeth's favorite, has the honor of making pipe smoking popular and respectable at the English court, from where it was eventually to spread rapidly to Europe and beyond. He had persuaded the queen herself to try a pipe—over which she spluttered to such an extent that his rival, the Earl of Essex, sought to convince Elizabeth that it was an attempt on her life. On another occasion the gardener, who came across Sir Walter smoking in his house, emptied a bucket of water over him

**Sixteenth-century gallants enjoy their "little ladles" in a tobacco club.**

to put out the fire. The gallant adventurer survived both these incidents only to be imprisoned and condemned to death by James I. It is said that he "tooke a pipe of tobacco a little before he went to the scaffolde."

There is no better way to end this glimpse of the discovery of tobacco than by quoting from Ben Jonson's play of 1598, *Every Man in His Humour*, in which his Captain Bobadil says:

> *"Sir, believe me upon my relation, for what I tell you the world shall not reprove, I have been to the Indies where Tobacco grows, where neither myself, nor a dozen gentlemen more of myself, have received the taste of any other nutriment in the world for the space of one and twenty weeks but the fume of this simple only. Therefore it cannot be but it is most divine."*

The Queen was not amused: Elizabeth I was said to have tried a pipe of tobacco but found it not to her taste.

Gallant Sir Walter Raleigh inspired such devotion in his servants that they would douse his face when it was on fire.

*"Sublime tobacco! which from east to west*
*Cheers the tar's labour or the Turkman's rest*
*Divine in hookas, glorious in a pipe*
*When tipp'd with amber, mellow, rich and ripe."*

The Island: Lord Byron, 1823

CHAPTER TWO

# The Habit Spreads

No longer the secret delight of the wealthy adventurer, by the start of the seventeenth century the habit of pipe smoking had spread to the ordinary man. In this tavern scene by the Dutch painter Adriaen van Ostade, a villager contemplates life with his simple pipe of clay and tobacco tin.

The sixteenth and seventeenth centuries were the period of the great maritime expansion of Western Europe. Its nations competed in trade for the exotic produce of the New World, and its ships' companies carried with them the seeds and secrets of the new American plant. Sea captain and seaman, merchant and ambassador, slave and slave trader, they all passed on the practice of the secret delight, whether as the solace for the toiler or the stimulus of kings.

The Portuguese, led around the Cape of Good Hope by Vasco da Gama, were active in the exploration of South America, Africa, and the East. The natural trade wind sailing route for their Far Eastern empire took them to the Brazilian coast from where tobacco could be procured, and from there they carried it to the four corners of the earth. They took it to India, the East Indies, and Japan from where it was introduced to Manchuria and north China; it reached south China from the Portuguese settlement at Macau. From these bases, the habit of smoking spread into Asia, where there was a practice of using a pipe with

Title page of a 1623 Dutch treatise on the subject of tobacco smoking.

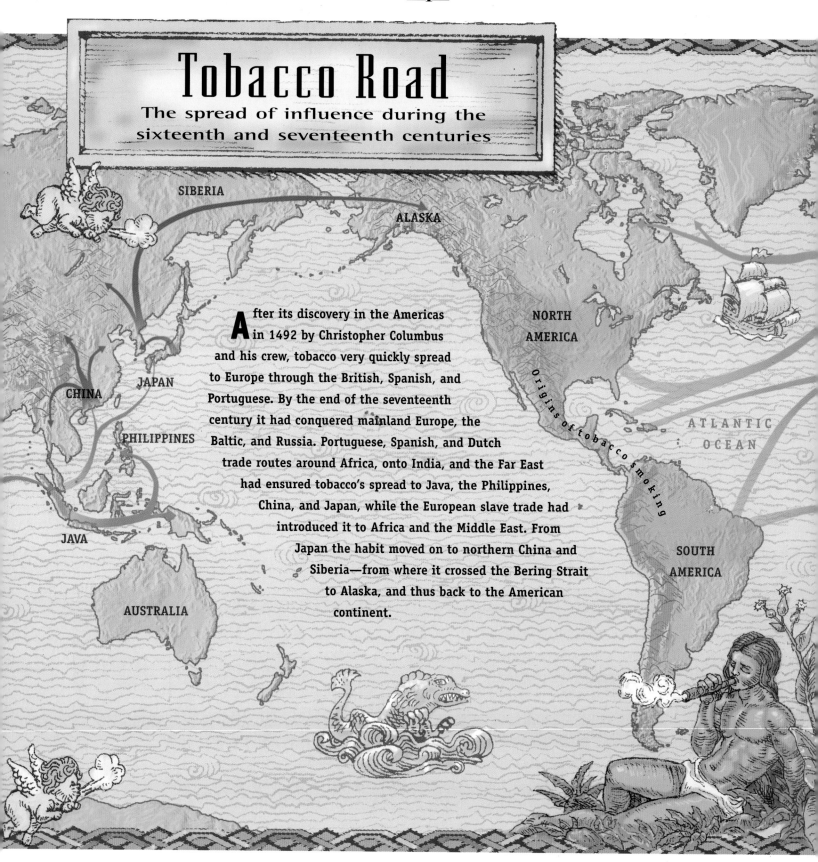

# Pipe

# Tobacco Road

## The spread of influence during the sixteenth and seventeenth centuries

SIBERIA

ALASKA

JAPAN

CHINA

PHILIPPINES

JAVA

AUSTRALIA

NORTH AMERICA

*Origins of tobacco smoking*

ATLANTIC OCEAN

SOUTH AMERICA

**A**fter its discovery in the Americas in 1492 by Christopher Columbus and his crew, tobacco very quickly spread to Europe through the British, Spanish, and Portuguese. By the end of the seventeenth century it had conquered mainland Europe, the Baltic, and Russia. Portuguese, Spanish, and Dutch trade routes around Africa, onto India, and the Far East had ensured tobacco's spread to Java, the Philippines, China, and Japan, while the European slave trade had introduced it to Africa and the Middle East. From Japan the habit moved on to northern China and Siberia—from where it crossed the Bering Strait to Alaska, and thus back to the American continent.

# Pipe

a small bowl, perhaps the legacy of inhaling hemp and the forerunner of the opium pipe. Ironically, the custom so entrenched among the North American Indians as a whole eventually reached the Indian tribes of Alaska from the "old world," across the Bering Strait from Russia.

The Dutch brought the plant and the use of it to South Africa where they established a station at the Cape of Good Hope. Here, the practice of inhaling the rough fumes of cannabis from earthen hearths had further developed: to cool the fumes, the Africans had devised a method of smoking whereby the smoke was drawn either through or across water. The Dutch at the Cape found the native Hottentots using an antelope horn as a stem filled with water from

**Two Japanese courtesans enjoy a stroll while showing off their long, elegant pipes.**

which a short length of hollow wood led to a stone bowl containing the leaf. They reported that the natives swiftly took to the newfangled tobacco, or a mixture of dakka and tobacco, and adopted the Dutch-style pipe. The women could be seen smoking freely and would offer the last whiff of their pipes to the child at their breast.

Arab slave traders may have become familiar with the more traditional manner of smoking dakka through water, and from it they contrived the use of the hollow nut of the coconut palm as the holder of water. Hence the name of nargileh or coconut for the simpler water pipes. This practice, too, spread along the new trade routes of the world.

Sir Thomas Roe, English ambassador to the Indian Mogul's court, described the smoking of the Persian water pipe, the kalian, writing in 1615:

*"Their way of taking it [tobacco] is something odd and strange, tho' perhaps they don't fire their mouths by it as*

# Pipe

**Looking supremely relaxed, a Chinese sailor smokes his long-stemmed pipe in his junk.**

*much as we do; for they take a little narrow-necked pot (that has an open round top, and a spout coming out of the belly on't) and fill it with water up to the lower part of the spout; then they lay their tobacco loose in the top of the pot, and upon it a Coal of fire, and so with a reed or Cane of an Ell long (which is inserted into the spout) they draw the Smoak into their mouths. They say it is much more cool and wholesome to do it thus than as the Europeans do, since all the smoak falls upon the surface of the Water before it passes into the Cane. The Tobacco of this country is thought to be as good as any in the World."*

This three-piece system was adopted extensively in Africa and the Middle East in different forms. Essentially, there was the bowl of stone or wood that held the glowing herb, the pot that contained water, and the pipe stem through which the smoker drew the smoke that had been cooled by passing across or through the water. This system was particularly suited to taking the raw heat out of the fumes of hemp or any mixture of

**Waiting for custom: a Turkish trader enjoys his pipe.**

it with the increasingly fashionable tobacco.

We know these pipes under the names of the hookah and the hubblebubble, the latter having the social advantage that a number of people might smoke using different tubes from a common bowl. But they existed in many unsophisticated forms, using gourds or horns to hold the water. A recent explorer of Arabia, Michael Asher, writes in the *Last of the Bedu: In Search of the Myth* of the present-day inhabitants of Shibam:

**Using water pipes, smokers in the Indian Mogul's court took their pleasures seriously.**

*"Piratical men sat around it [the square] smoking water pipes made from bean-cans and old coconut shells."* An emaciated old man *"pulled the pipe shakily towards him, then took his own tobacco from his pocket and unwrapped it. He rubbed and rolled it steadily with the ease of long practice, then lifted the pot of his pipe and filled it with unhurried grace. He sat for a moment in contemplation of it. There was all the time in the world to enjoy this pleasure. The tea-boy leaned over with a piece of charcoal on a pincer. The old man planted the stem loosely in a hole drilled in the coconut-shell. He took a deep toke, coughed, spluttered, then toked again. His shrunken face lit up with pleasure as the smoke trickled back out of his mouth and nostrils."*

The Koran was written too early to contain any prohibition on smoking, although the more devout Muslim may prefer the tobacco not to touch his lips, thus giving encouragement to the pipe, and the water pipe in particular.

# ℙipe

## Cure-All Solution

Thus the trading ships from the ports of coastal Europe spread pipe smoking throughout the world: the Spanish and Portuguese to the Far East and West Africa, the Dutch to the Cape and the Indies, the Venetians to the Levant and the English into the Baltic and to Russia. Yet the habit penetrated at first very slowly into mainland Europe itself, where tobacco, which Jean Nicot had disseminated, was in general regarded only as a plant with medicinal properties.

Seventeenth-century physician Johannes Vittich, wrote:

*"There can be no doubt that tobacco can cleanse all impurities and disperse every grave and viscous humor, as we find by daily experience."*

*"It cures cancer of the breast, open sores, scabs, scratches, however poisonous and septic, goitre, broken limbs, erysipelas, and many other things. It will heal wounds in the arms and legs and other members of the body of however long standing. The place must first be bathed with white wine or urine and wiped clean with a sponge or rag, one or two fresh leaves must then be pounded together with the juice and applied to the wound with a white napkin to protect it, the treatment to be continued until the cure be complete."*

To the list of ailments *nicotiana* was thought to cure was added syphilis, allegedly brought back from the Indies by the same importers of the plant. More important, the smoke from the pipe was seen as a protection against epidemics such as the plague and cholera.

This worthy medical attitude toward tobacco and the smoke it produced was, however, not destined to reign supreme. Whether it first reached the European mainland through the contact with

**16th century Dutch physician Gilles Everaerts evidently worried little about any health hazard from pipe smoking.**

**Following Jean Nicot's lead, physicians and alchemists all over Europe eagerly delved into the healing properties of the tobacco leaf.**

# Pipe

Europe in the 16th and 17th centuries, with its poor standards of public hygiene, fell prey to frequent epidemics, like the plague and cholera.

Fear of these outbreaks of killer diseases fostered desperate ideas of how to protect the populace, and assiduous smoking of a pipe was widely believed to stave off having to join the many corpses in the mass burial pits.

The Thirty Years War ravaged Europe, but was instrumental in the spread of tobacco and the pipe.

students at Leyden University or seamen at the ports, the habit of smoking that was so prevalent in England would at last sweep across the Channel and inland, carried by the armies of the Thirty Years War (1618–1648), whose main preoccupation with tobacco was the pleasure it afforded.

The war that set Catholics against Protestants among countries struggling for independence involved almost all the European powers and their mercenary armies. As they marched and countermarched across the continent, the populace observed their strange habit of "drinking tobacco" and swiftly adopted it for themselves. Already cultivated as a garden plant, the thousand tiny seeds that it yields were soon growing for other, even more pleasing purposes in small holdings from Holland to Hungary, and from Switzerland to Sweden.

Smoking it in a pipe is not, of course, the only use to which tobacco is put. The Elizabethans were already familiar with the American customs of chewing and snuff taking as well as smoking "the little ladles." Although in the seventeenth century adventurous ladies tried their hands at the clay pipe, their eighteenth-century counterparts appeared much happier with the more elegant habit of taking snuff, turning readily to the deco-

**By the end of the Thirty Years War, people could relax over a drink in a small Belgian tavern and enjoy a smoke of tobacco grown in its back yard.**

rated snuff boxes that allowed them to display their ringed fingers as they toyed with them.

Despite the endless objections of kings and princes, the habit

spread unstoppably among all classes of society. The rulers could argue that it was medically useless and indeed damaging to health, that it was dangerous in causing serious fires among the wooden buildings of the towns, that it was un-Christian and the practice of the heathen, that it was dirty and obstructed work—they could present any argument they liked, but pipe smoking steadily increased. It would not be too fanciful a notion to imagine that a scavenger on the battlefield outside the gates of Vienna, where the Turks were defeated in 1683, might have found among the bodies of the soldiers the broken fragments of a Western clay pipe, the shards of a levantine hookah, or even pieces of the small-bowled Asiatic pipe.

**One of the more adventurous sixteenth-century ladies drinking from both cup and pipe.**

Nonetheless, official hostility to tobacco smoking continued to strengthen, until, by the middle of the seventeenth century, just as governments were forced to acknowledge that the habit was so firmly and popularly established that they could not prevent it, the clever idea would arise of looking to this vice for a source of income—a paradoxical practice that would continue, as inexorably and universally as smoking itself, to the present day.

**The contemplative young smoker of Europe lights up in this seventeenth-century French painting after Georges de La Tour.**

**A**rt often reflects everyday life, and the paintings from northern Europe in the seventeenth century demonstrate just how complete the acceptance of pipe smoking had become. Numerous still lives include clay pipes and tobacco in their artfully arranged displays of common household paraphernalia. Portraits and numerous tavern scenes attest to the popularity of smoking with the ordinary folk, both young and old. The pipe and its use also provided ample inspiration for the painters of the then popular fantasies, such as the anthropomorphic monkeys disporting their love of smoking in the picture above.

Right: "Still life with jug, and clay pipes" by Hubert van Ravenstyn (1638–91); and inset: "Still life with beer glass and clay pipes" by Jan III Van De Velde (c1620-62)

Opposite page; top: "Tobacco club for monkeys" by Abraham Teniers (1629–70); bottom: "Vanitas" by Pieter Van Steenwyck (17th century)

# $\mathbb{P}$ipe

*"Put out that light!"*

Air-raid warden's cry in London's wartime blackout

CHAPTER THREE

# Challengers

From the earliest times of smoking there have been those who simply loathed it, and the list of those in authority who sought to ban the habit is long.

King James I, almost as soon as he ascended to the joint thrones of England and Scotland, began the onslaught with the publication in 1604 of *A Counterblaste to Tobacco*. He was prudent enough to issue the work anonymously, although everyone knew who wrote it. He ended his attack:

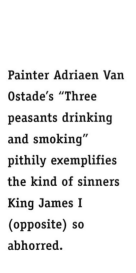

Painter Adriaen Van Ostade's "Three peasants drinking and smoking" pithily exemplifies the kind of sinners King James I (opposite) so abhorred.

*"In your abuse thereof sinning against God, harming yourselves both in persons and goods... by the custome thereof making your selves to be wondered at by all forraine civil Nations, and by all strangers that come among you, to be scorned and contemned. A custome lothsome to the eye, hatefull to the nose, harmful to the braine, dangerous to the Lungs, and in the black, stinking fume thereof, nearest resembling the horrible Stigian smoke of the pit that is bottomlesse."*

In this powerful and scholarly royal sweep he encompassed all the objections—religious, personal, medical, and economic—that continue to be made today.

And yet, by the time King James launched his thunderous blast it was already too late. The habit of smoking was widespread in his kingdom; foreigners commented on the extent to which the country was possessed by it, even, it was said, in the new theaters. The smoking of clay pipes had become the practice of the countryman and the courtier.

Charles I followed his father in disliking smoking and instigated further hostile laws that no one obeyed, and he himself was mocked by the Cromwellian soldiers guarding him in prison who blew smoke in his face and then threw broken pipes at him on his way to the scaffold.

**Like his father, Charles I may have disapproved of the smoking habit, but his Cavaliers certainly seemed to take up the pipe at a young age (right).**

As the habit of smoking spread across Europe with the Thirty Years War, the authorities reacted against it. While the Church had to face the difficulty that, not unnaturally, the Bible offered no guidance on the subject, the habit looked too much like a pleasurable vice for it to be accepted. As early as the sixteenth century one unfortunate Spaniard found with smoke coming out of his mouth and nostrils was duly considered to be in league with the devil and thrown into prison. Official disapproval came when excessive snuff taking and smoking in the cathedral in Seville during Mass led Pope Urban VIII to issue a formal decree against it. The growing appeal of smoking was, however, amply demonstrated

**Pope Urban VIII— one of the first to legislate against smoking in a public meeting place.**

when a later pope gave it his blessing, converted to the virtue of fellowship in the sharing of tobacco in Saint Peter's in Rome itself.

### Permission Denied

The sultans in Constantinople reacted more violently. Smokers had their pipes thrust through their noses or were otherwise mutilated. Murad IV (not surprisingly known as the Cruel) would wander the streets to find those enjoying tobacco in secret and have them executed the following day and their goods forfeited. It was not until later that his successors, realizing the special advantages of the Turkish climate for growing tobacco, relaxed their persecutions. The users of the hookah and hubblebubble could relax.

Czar Michael in Russia was just as brutal as the Turkish sultan. Encouraged by his father, the patriarch of the Church, who objected strongly to smoking during services, Michael punished transgressors by slitting their lips or flogging by the knout, which was often fatal, as the whip was tipped with three thongs of raw elkskin. Not until Peter the Great became czar could the Russians smoke freely—Peter had acquired the habit of the pipe in the Dutch shipyards.

In Japan, where even the geishas took to it, and other countries, draconian laws were passed against smoking, and informants were encouraged to report offenders by being handsomely rewarded for their efforts.

Frequently the ruler laid down the danger of fire as the reason for his ban. Clearly, in an age when houses were built of mostly wood and the light for the tobacco was smoldering charcoal, the smoker could be easily, and perhaps not unfairly, condemned.

**Firefighters attempt to put out a fire in the center of Amsterdam—it's not said that this one was started by a pipe smoker, but they often were.**

**Amurath (Murad), who ruled as Sultan of Constantinople from 1623–40, not content to sit back and let others enforce his smoking ban, actively sought out wrongdoers.**

# Pipe

Napoleon objected to one of his generals smoking, berating him for smelling so much of tobacco that no woman in Paris would come near him. (The emperor himself was a lover of snuff.) His enemy, the Duke of Wellington, took his officers to task for smoking and circulated to the regiments a formal letter of discouragement.

Frederick the Great so hated it that he forbade it in Germany in 1764. His decree made it illegal to smoke in the Berlin streets and in the Tiergarten, which the king had made into a public park. Other more dangerous places such as joiners' workshops were included in the ban because of the risk of setting fire to the shavings on the floor. The police harried the workmen enthusiastically, since a handsome reward was paid for a successful prosecution.

Frederick the Great (Friedrich II, 1712–1786) banned an entire city from the smoking of pipes.

These laws stayed in place until the early nineteenth century. When Napoleon's troops occupied Berlin, the rules lapsed as the French did not obey them, but as soon as they were gone the prohibition was reestablished. The chief of police issued an order on June 8, 1810, stating that:

Napoleon, who hated smoking but enjoyed snuff, is seen here appropriately decorating the lid of snuff box.

*"seeing that public smoking in streets and on promenades is as indecent as it is dangerous, and contrary to the character of an orderly and civilized city, the same is hereby strictly forbidden, not only for Berlin, but in Charlottenburg and the Tiergarten, and may only take place in the two latter places at the doors of houses, on the part of those who sit and stand there. Anyone transgressing shall be arrested, his pipe shall be taken away, and he shall be punished with a fine, or corresponding imprisonment or corporal punishment."*

The working man resented the law that the royal governor, von Tippelkirsch, continued to enforce strictly. In 1831 there was an outbreak of cholera in Berlin, and for a time the ban was lifted because smoking was regarded as a protection against the disease, after which all manner of populace, from boys to men, were

**Smokers, repressed on the streets of Berlin, might have envied their counterparts in "The club smoking room" in Vienna.**

seen strolling around the streets with flaming cigars or uncovered pipes in a defiant gesture of freedom.

When the epidemic passed, von Tippelkirsch was successful in reinforcing the law. He rode out each morning in the Tiergarten hunting down offenders whose pipes he considered the symbols of the revolutionary. In a return of the disease in 1837, restrictions were again lifted only to be reissued by the intolerant von Tippelkirsch.

The populace remained defiant. In 1846, the complaint of the authorities was that there had only been 3,712 prosecutions. Finally the democrats of Berlin gained their freedom to smoke in the Tiergarten in the tide of revolution that swept across Europe in 1848.

In Great Britain, Queen Victoria would not tolerate the polluting habit at Windsor, where ministers summoned to her

The tide of revolution that swept Europe in 1848 brought riots to the streets of Berlin. While the aim of the liberals was political reform in Prussia, the new constitution forced on King Frederick William IV also brought in its wake the long-denied freedom to smoke .

# Pipe

presence could only smoke surreptitiously up the chimney (fore-runners, perhaps, of contemporary cigarette smokers forced to skulk in the doorways of nonsmoking bars and restaurants). In America, Henry Ford was another who could not abide the smell of smoke, and he tried to keep his car manufacturing plants non-smoking. Nazi tyrant Adolf Hitler said to his mistress, Eva Braun, "Either give up smoking or me."

In the United States the authoritarian backlash against lighting up occurred late. The early settlers and planters had happily smoked with the Indians, and it was not until the last quarter of the nineteenth century that state governments started to pass restrictive laws, primarily aimed at the cigarette. But without the support of the federal government and against the popular enthusiasm for smoking, these laws were generally ignored and ultimately repealed.

Henry Ford, who could be said to have invented mass-produced pollution, tried to keep his automotive manufacturing plants smoke-free zones.

From the beginning, it was the same strength of public opinion that challenged lawmakers throughout the world. Faced by what King James had been unable to stop in Great Britain, his brother rulers abroad found themselves equally ineffectual, as pipe smoking established itself everywhere.

Today, once more, smoking encounters opposition from those in authority, a development reinforced by a shift in public opinion that has been swayed by a barrage of media reporting on the health risks from pursuing the habit. Although the focus is mainly on the harmful consumption of cigarettes, it cannot be denied that even the long-established, civilized tradition of the pipe falls under the sober pall emanating from those who would tell us what is good for us.

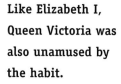

Like Elizabeth I, Queen Victoria was also unamused by the habit.

The White House is now a smoke-free zone, and everywhere in the modern world we are confronted with "No Smoking" signs—

the quintessential symbols of repression of individual freedom for a large segment of the population.

Legislators and antismoking lobbyists might do well to contemplate the opinion expressed by English professor Roger Scruton in an article of late 1997 published in Britain's *The Times* newspaper:

> *"Properly used, tobacco makes a real and positive contribution to health. It calms the nerves and imposes moments of rest and contemplation; it also equips people for the trials of social life by providing something which can be offered and accepted at any time of day. It is from the American pipe of peace that we learnt to smoke. Our ancestors perceived the great moral and social benefits that the Indians obtained from this source, and were wise enough to bring it home with them."*

Amen, the pipe smoker might like to add.

"Properly used... tobacco calms the nerves and imposes moments of rest and contemplation." A relaxing 1859 painting by the appropriately-named François Bonvin.

# ᴘipe

## The Smoke of War

In the spread and changes of tobacco habits there has often been a striking connection with war, and the arrival of snuff in England and Germany was no exception. Soldiers of the armies engaged in the Thirty Years War had carried the practice of pipe smoking to every corner of Europe. In the English Civil War, both the Royalists and the Roundheads smoked—perhaps the absence of biblical condemnation was taken by the Puritans as consent. But when Charles II was restored to the throne in 1660, he and his courtiers brought with them the French court's habit of snuff taking. By the time of Queen Anne, the last of the Stewart monarchs, pipe smoking was banished to the middle and working classes, and in high society snuff reigned supreme, leading the English poet William Cowper to somewhat wistfully write:

*Says the pipe to the snuffbox I can't understand*
*What the ladies and gentleman see in your face*
*That you are in fashion all over the land*
*And I am so much fallen in disgrace.*

**Top: France started the fashion for taking snuff in the seventeenth century and it continued well into the nineteenth, as the French ladies of 1824 prove. Below: a typical decorated snuff box of the time.**

At the end of the century and the beginning of the nineteenth, the Napoleonic Wars acted as a vector for another form of smoking: the cigar. The Spanish people, never greatly taken by the pipe, had always preferred the "golden tubes" of the Indies. The British, French, and the other continental forces fighting in the Peninsula took this novel practice home with them.

Forty years later, as a new generation of aristocratic officers "like Mars, a smoking their pipes and cigars" went with the common soldiery and their clays to the Crimean War, a smaller, thinner instrument was evolved as a means for a swifter smoke, and in turn its use was spread in the United States by the Civil War. The cigarette had arrived.

Along with the cigarette came a way of lighting it easily with the sulphur match. It was the beginning of the end for the clay pipe that for three hundred years had been a cheap and

**Crimean War (1853–56): pioneer photographer Roger Fenton's plate shows General Ismael Pasha, who fought for the British, being handed a clay pipe in a break between hostilities.**

discardable purveyor of smoke, lit by charcoal tongs or candle. By 1900, cigarette factories were catering for a mass market.

Finally, World Wars I and II saw the establishment of the supremacy of the newcomer. The descendants of those who had found solace in their pipes now took comfort from their Lucky Strikes and Woodbines. The cigarette became the symbol of comradeship and shared hardship, as portrayed endlessly in Hollywood movies. U.S. General Pershing, in World War I, is recorded as saying that his boys had to have their tobacco. Equally the women at home and in the factories demanded theirs.

In the same way in World War II, tobacco had to come up with the rations in every theater of the conflict and in the Red Cross consignments for prisoner-of-war camps as well. Warfare once again had confirmed us in our smoking habits.

**A World War I cigarette advertisement enters into the patriotic spirit.**

# Pipe

# Pipe

A World War I English warrior lights a cigarette in the night.

## The Taxman Cometh

A cynical cardinal once said, "God desireth not the death of a sinner but rather that he should live and pay." When rulers found that they could not prevent the use of tobacco, they swiftly realized that it was a source of revenue. To begin with, the government profited from fines as well as import taxes. The duty imposed on imported tobacco by Queen Elizabeth at twopence a pound was increased fortyfold by King James I. At such a price no wonder the bowls of the early clay pipes were small, and one can only presume that the rapid spread of the habit was based on smuggling. Indeed, as early as 1597 records show that American tobacco was being smuggled into Cornwall in large quantities by French, Flemish, and Cornish ships.

*Nicotiana tabacum* is a tolerant plant that will grow in most temperate climates. Historically in England, home cultivation was alternately banned or heavily taxed: King Charles II sent his cavalry into the fields to ride down the crops, and as late as 1782, in George III's reign, plantations in Yorkshire were destroyed by troops and the growers heavily fined and imprisoned. In present-day Britain, unlike the United States, tobacco is not a commercial crop. The rules are that you may grow it yourself, and what you grow is for your own use and you may not sell it.

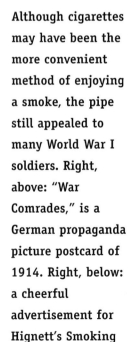

Although cigarettes may have been the more convenient method of enjoying a smoke, the pipe still appealed to many World War I soldiers. Right, above: "War Comrades," is a German propaganda picture postcard of 1914. Right, below: a cheerful advertisement for Hignett's Smoking Mixture.

In seventeenth-century Europe kings and princes wrestled with the moral dilemma of making money from what most of them disapproved of. All manner of laws were made in an effort to prevent or limit the habit. In Switzerland for a time, the individual smoker had to pay an annual tax, rather like a dog license. Not surprisingly these and all other efforts failed. Farmers continued to grow the crop, and men, women, and children to smoke it.

Even in the United States, home to the plant, a few early Puritan laws were passed against its use. In Connecticut, for example, a man was allowed one pipe a day or on a journey one pipe in every ten miles he traveled, with fines for offending.

HIGNETT'S SMOKING MIXTURE

"THE RIGHT STUFF"

# Pipe

The cigarette became the symbol of comradeship and shared hardship. Two young Wehrmacht soldiers during a lull in the fighting on the Eastern front, April 1942...

...while on the Western front only two years later, an American GI advances in France.

By 1648 most European countries had legislation forbidding smoking. And yet, within a mere ten years a much more profitable, and therefore preferable, alternative solution had been found: the monopoly. While some governments experimented by giving themselves sole rights to deal in tobacco, it fell to Venice to devise the easiest and most lucrative system, whereby a merchant acquired from the government, at a high price, the exclusive right to import, manufacture, and trade. Appalto, as it was called, quickly became the model for other countries.

In different and increasingly onerous forms the state has raised revenue from tobacco for four hundred years. Currently every country in Europe taxes tobacco, with the United Kingdom almost at the head of the league table. In the United States not only the federal government but also the individual states tax it. In 1891 the British government took a total of $15.8 million (£9.9 million) from tobacco. In 1997 it took $16 billion (£10 billion), or about 2.8 percent of its total revenue.

# P̲i̲p̲e̲

The federal government in the United States began to tax tobac-co in 1864 and the individual states later, with the six highest currently being California, Texas, New York, New Jersey, Illinois, and Washington. Tobacco is naturally much cheaper in the United States where a citizen can earn the cost of a smoke in half the time of a Briton.

It comes as no surprise then, that with the different systems of taxation in modern countries, smuggling continues on as large a scale today as it ever did in the past. The U.S. federal govern-ment alone may lose $320 million a year, and in Britain it is estimated to cost the treasury half a billion pounds annually.

**A sign of the times: Keep 'em Smokin' may have been an acceptable slogan for World War II's fighting men, but sixty years later, it is the cigarette companies who are at war against popular feeling.**

# Pipe

*"Lastly, (and this is perhaps the golden rule), no woman should marry a teetotaller or a man who does not smoke."*

Virginibus Puerisque, Robert Louis Stevenson, 1891

CHAPTER FOUR

# The Pipe Smoker

Smoking a pipe, as indeed any form of smoking, is a not just a pleasurable activity, it's a style statement, and defines the character of the smoker. Therefore the image of the smoker has always been important: the addition of an artifact to the mouth and the way that it is handled conveys a message and can create a role model to aspire to. In times of greater latitude, there appeared little wrong in the young emulating their elders (and betters), and for young boys to smoke was often a means of looking tougher and more grown up.

In Europe during the early years of the habit, instances are given of entire families smoking, and, as we have seen, at times of epidemics everyone was encouraged to do so; indeed, in one often-quoted occasion the boys at Eton College were ordered to! Since then, of course, the orders have more commonly been the reverse.

There are two classic accounts in fiction of the young modeling themselves on their elders, one by Mark Twain and the other by Rudyard Kipling. In Mark Twain's *The Adventures of Tom Sawyer* we learn that:

*Tom said he wanted to learn to smoke now. Joe caught at the idea and said he would like to try too. So Huck made pipes*

**Young acolytes of the pipe: Tom Sawyer and pal Joe puff knowledgeably on their corncobs while bragging of their exploits in Mark Twain's The Adventures of Tom Sawyer.**

Mark Twain (SL Clements) and pipe as seen in Vanity Fair, 1908.

*and filled them. These novices had never smoked anything before but cigars made of grapevine, and they "bit" the tongue and were not considered manly anyway.*

*Now they stretched themselves out on their elbows and began to puff charily and with slender confidence. The smoke had an unpleasant taste and they gagged a little but Tom said:*

*"Why, it's just as easy. If I'd a knowed this was all, I'd a learnt long ago."*

*"So would I," said Joe. "It's just nothing."*

*"Why, many a time I've just looked at people smoking and thought, well I wish I could do that; but I never thought I could," said Tom.*

*Both boys were looking pale and miserable now. Joe's pipe dropped from his nerveless fingers, Tom's followed.*

In *Stalky & Co* Rudyard Kipling wrote:

*In summer all right-minded boys built huts in the furze hill behind the College—little lairs whittled out of the heart of the prickly bushes, full of stumps, odd root-ends, and spikes, but, since they were strictly forbidden, palaces of delight. And for the fifth summer in succession, Stalky, McTurk and Beetle (this was before they reached the dignity of a study)*

Emulating their elders: this unique pipe, once the property of the Emperor of Austria, depicts the experiences of eight youngsters smoking for the first time

*had built like beavers a place of retreat and meditation, where they smoked.*

Kipling based his character of Stalky on a boy called Dunsterville who rose to be a major general. He recalled in his memoirs using clay pipes and shag in their hideaway, which made them very sick. He continued, however, as one of the many military pipe smokers in British India.

For the adult the pipe may be expected to be more pleasurable than Tom's or Stalky's. Yet the smoking of tobacco has an effect that varies with each individual since what is drawn in can be a stimulus or a tranquilizer: it can be the prelude to action or set the body to rest. The image of the pipe smoker can therefore be of the active explorer or the thoughtful philosopher, Sir Ranulph Fiennes or Jean Paul Sartre.

The pipe is an awkward instrument to use at the height of action, up the mast or on the battlefield, so that even for the man of deeds there is a suggestion that he smokes it in preparation or in giving an account of the day as evening falls. In contrast, when the thinker blows a meditative smoke ring, the tobacco lulls the body as the mind sets out on its adventures.

At different times when pipes were all the rage, different images must have been presented. The Elizabethan ploughman making a crude bowl from a walnut shell and a stem from a reed or selecting a newfangled clay from a passing peddler may have felt himself like a courtier experimenting with a silver pipe—the feeling of excitement in an age of discovery. They might each also have enjoyed the tasting of forbidden fruits in the face of the king's disapproval.

## Into Action

The soldiers who spread the habit across Europe must have carried with them the same sense of adventure as well as hardship endured, offering to the inhabitants of the lands they traversed

The thinker: for Jean Paul Sartre, smoking his pipe (and a good many cigarettes, too) was a stimulus during the action...

...but for men of action, the pipe is reserved for contemplative moments before or after the battle.

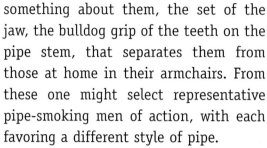

Defiant and powerful: General Douglas MacArthur pictured with his unmistakeable corncob pipe.

an example quickly followed. "It is a common saying that if a man is not a lusty smoker, he is no true soldier, indeed hardly a man at all," wrote one observer at the time of the Thirty Years War.

Historically a host of people engaged in manly pursuits with which the pipe is firmly associated: soldiers and sailors, explorers and prospectors, frontiersmen and empire builders. There is something about them, the set of the jaw, the bulldog grip of the teeth on the pipe stem, that separates them from those at home in their armchairs. From these one might select representative pipe-smoking men of action, with each favoring a different style of pipe.

Douglas MacArthur was one of the great generals of the twentieth century. In World War I he was in charge of the American Rainbow Division and decorated thirteen times. In World War II he recaptured the Philippines, as supreme commander of the South-West Pacific Area accepted the Japanese surrender on the battleship Missouri, and then governed the defeated Japan. He went on to command the United Nations forces in the Korean War. In his photographs he stands defiant and powerful with an unusual pipe in his mouth, the unmistakable corncob.

Another soldier one might pick is the German swashbuckling cavalry officer, Gebhard Leberecht von Blucher, Prince of Wahlstadt, who was nicknamed "Marshal Forward." He was dismissed from the Prussian army in his youth for insubordination and dissipation but was later recalled to take command and harry Napoleon into exile. A handsome mustachioed figure, in his pictures he is rarely seen without a pipe with a long stem and short mouthpiece, perhaps a porcelain one from Meissen. He is chiefly known in military history for turning up late (but effectively) at the battle of Waterloo.

THE SATURDAY EVENING POST

An Illustrated Weekly
Founded A.D. 1728 by Benj. Franklin

JAN. 18, 1919        5c. THE COPY        10c. in Canada

Pipe-smoking Houdini: British air ace Sir Douglas Bader never gave up trying to escape POW camps. In the incident that brought his fighter down over France and placed him the hands of the occupying forces, when one artificial leg became trapped, he jumped, leaving it behind.

One would also want a frontiersman: Mose Milner was fortunate enough not to reach his battlefield at all. Nicknamed "California Joe," he was a scout for General George Armstrong Custer who asked him to join the expedition to Montana. Mose begged off because he had run out of tobacco and so escaped the encounter at Little Big Horn. He must have been happy enough to recount the tale over the campfire for years to come, smoking the rough and bent wooden pipe he is shown with in the one existing photograph of him.

Sir Douglas Bader, the much decorated English airman, lost both his legs in an air accident before World War II and then learned to fly again with the aid of artificial ones. He led the first Royal Air Force Canadian Fighter Squadron until he collided with an enemy aircraft over France, parachuted to the ground, and was taken prisoner of war. Because of his numerous escape attempts, the Germans removed his prosthetic legs and sent him

The solace of the pipe: artist Norman Rockwell captures the image of the strong-but-quiet man of action in this *Saturday Evening Post Cover* of 1919.

**Of course, the fact that a man smokes a pipe doesn't guarantee his pleasantness—Joseph Stalin was responsible for millions of deaths.**

to the infamous Colditz Castle POW camp. After the war he dedicated his life to the service of the disabled. When photographed he is always seen gently balanced on his tin pins with a briar pipe in his mouth, even playing golf.

It would be pleasant to record that dictators are not associated with pipes. We have seen that Hitler detested tobacco, and, after an attempt as incompetent as Tom Sawyer's, Napoleon disapproved of smoking. However, Joseph Stalin smoked his Russian pipe during the times when he was responsible for the deaths of millions of his countrymen. In later years, he told Winston Churchill that he was taking up cigars.

While popular with all the services at war, tobacco has always been of special importance to the sailor, something to allay the traditional hardship of the sea and to comfort him off watch. In the British Navy the break announced by the bosun's call as "Stand easy" is ended by "Out pipes." You have the vision of a bearded figure struggling in a gale to light his "short clay," such

**A sea-battered coast guardsman, clenches his pipe in grim determination.**

as Popeye carries in his mouth as a fixture, or spinning yarns over it at the Sailors' Rest in the evening. The seaman has always had the advantage in life in getting his tobacco duty-free and on occasion, as of old, smuggling it ashore with him.

**In times of hardship, the shared pipe brokered a deep sense of comradeship.**

There is also, as many point out, a deep sense of

# Pipe

comradeship in the habit. It was due to such a deep-seated feeling that the London Pipe-makers' Guild motto was "Let brother love continue." The shared pipe, the shared tobacco, the shared light, be it from charcoal, candle, or match, supply a bond that modern life loses. Wartime pictures recall many scenes of shared hardships and the shared smoke.

The pipe, unlike its rivals, is still there after its tobacco has gone, to be reused, and remains as a constant friend, sometimes rather unkindly seen as a mother substitute. As a companion for the solitary or a bond of company it plays its part.

## To Smoke is to Think

If you might choose a practical pipe smoker for a partner in a desperate venture, you should not forget the merits of the great thinkers who have dreamed great visions behind their pipes.

Sir Isaac Newton, the expositor of gravity, for example, was a heavy smoker, though not always so gallant with the ladies. It is told of him that in an absent-minded moment when filling his pipe with tobacco, he seized the little finger of a girl sitting next to him and used it as stopper. Did the apple that fell on his head interrupt his afternoon pipe?

There are many figures of pipe-smoking academics, of whom the Oxford University dons are archetypal. The Canadian professor and humorist, Stephen Leacock, writes of an undergraduate who described his Oxford tutor, "We go over to his rooms and he just lights his pipe and talks to us." Leacock goes on: "From this and other evidence I gather that what an Oxford tutor does is to get a little group of students together and smoke at them. Men who have been systematically smoked at for four years turn into ripe scholars... A well-smoked man speaks and writes English

Blowing bubbles: Sir Isaac Newton "studying" the effects of gravity in his garden, from a 1927 Swedish illustration.

A German student gazes dreamily into the future, taking inspiration from his elaborate pipe.

with a grace that can be acquired in no other way. His tutor will smoke at him until he kindles him into flame." (Nowadays the passive smoking lobby would be calling for his instant dismissal.)

James Thurber recalls his pipe-smoking English professor at Ohio State University, Joseph Russell Taylor, of whom the story was told that he began his lecture to one of his classes, "I do not expect you to take notes in this class." They all wrote it down! Taylor was well known for his pipe, and it was included in his portrait painted by George Bellows. It was hung in the Gallery of Fine Art in Columbus where it was known as Bellows's "Man with a Pipe." Taylor in his later years once asked Thurber whether he smoked while he wrote. Thurber, not wishing to disappoint the old man, replied that he did, but in fact he was a nonsmoker.

The academic has long been able to offer his wisdom from behind a screen of smoke. As William Cowper wrote in 1782:

German author Günther Grass looks quizzical.

> *The pipe with solemn interposing puff,*
> *Makes half a sentence at a time enough;*
> *The dozing sages drop the drowsy strain,*
> *Then pause, and puff—and speak and pause again.*

The cloud of blue smoke rising over the armchair may often have

Perhaps the ultimate thinking man of his time, Albert Einstein.

# Pipe

concealed the writer whose habits are known because he wrote about them. We know Milton liked a pipe after his evening meal. Carlyle, Thackeray, Tennyson, and Mark Twain (Samuel Clemens) all enjoyed their pipes, the latter calling himself a connoisseur of the cob (a pipe described later). Yet Izaac Walton, a keen smoker as well as fisherman, managed to write his famous *Compleat Angler or the Contemplative Man's Recreation* without once mentioning tobacco. And Shakespeare, although we know that his audiences smoked in the theater, said not a word on the subject.

Many artists have drawn their inspiration from a pipe of tobacco. From William Hogarth we have the sad picture of the artist himself in his last drawing, a broken pipe at his feet and, rather mischievously, a small coat of arms carrying Britannia and a lion each with a pipe in their mouths. The musicians George Friedrich Händel and Johann Sebastian Bach loved their pipes, the latter even composing a charming song entitled *Die Tabakspfeife* (*The Tobacco Pipe*).

William Hogarth's "A midnight modern conversation" combines the influences of both tobacco and punch.

# Pipe

Entitled "Malignant Aspects looking with envy on John Bull and his Satelites" (*sic*), or "A NEW PLANETARY SYSTEM", this 1807 engraving sums up the newly-smug, political Britain, lording it over envious "Johnny Foreigner," with John Bull as the image of pipe-smoking solidity.

## Piety, Wisdom, and Reliability

Popes may have banned pipes and then endorsed them, but an important source of Victorian wisdom in the heyday of the pipe was the clergy. Whereas some scorned it, many composed their sermons with its help in their vicarages and manses. On their pastoral rounds it gave them the image of reliability and, perhaps, the common touch. The rector and author of *The Water Babies*, Charles Kingsley, was seen one day extracting a pipe from a whin bush, and explained, when challenged, that he kept a scattering of pipes thus concealed around his parish as he never knew when he might want one.

# Pipe

Some have detected an air of eccentricity in pipe smoking, and nothing better describes the condition than the story of a nameless Lincolnshire curate who always retired to the vestry during the hymn prior to his sermon for a quick puff. When his clerk came to tell him that his congregation was waiting, he suggested that because he was not finished, they should sing another psalm.

"They've done that," replied the clerk.

"Then," said the curate, "let them sing psalm 119."

No doubt the congregation groaned as they commenced the longest psalm in the book at 176 verses, sufficient for several pipefuls.

An even more unlikely tale is told by Sir Walter Scott in his novel *The Heart of Midlothian*, bearing in mind that he generally took his scenes from real life. He relates that the Reverend Duncan of Knockdander, climbing to his pulpit to preach, produced a short iron pipe and exclaimed, "I hae forgotten my spleuchan [tobacco pouch], Lachlan, gang doon to the clachan and buy me a pennyworth of twist."

With the twentieth century, the John Bull spirit had become no less "bullish," but more sophisticated. The Conservative Prime Minister Stanley Baldwin's image of reliability was enhanced through his pipe and the bowler hat.

A member of his congregation immediately offered him tobacco, which he lit with a pistol flint and proceeded to smoke throughout his sermon of an hour and a quarter. At the end he knocked out his pipe (history does not say where), put it back in his sporran (a pouch traditionally worn with a kilt), and returned the spleuchan to its owner.

With the arrival in the nineteenth century of the meerschaum and the briar, there was a wide range of pipes to choose from. The clay might be all right for the artisan, but for the vicarage study and the smoking room at the club, a gentleman required a better class of pipe to give him the image of respectability. The cigarette was for upstarts and snuff taking for the old-fashioned.

# Pipe

"I shall be a gen'l'man myself one of these days, perhaps with a pipe in my mouth and a summerhouse in the back garden," says a character in Charles Dickens's *Pickwick Papers*.

Dickens was not a smoker himself and after a visit to the United States came back very shocked by the amount of cigarette smoking. He created, however, in his writing the picture of the contented and respectable family scene with the father of the household and his gentleman guests, the churchwardens, enjoying the long-stemmed clays and surrounded by adoring wife and children. Although Dickens was surely aware of the courtesy usually afforded to any ladies present, as the contemporary poet C. S. Calverley noted:

> *Jones (who I'm glad to say*
> *Asked leave of Mrs J.)*
> *Daily absorbs a clay*
> *After his labours.*

Politicians happily accepted the image of reliability that a pipe can give. Perhaps the British didn't trust Winston Churchill because of his cigar; it was somehow separative. On the other hand, Stanley Baldwin, three times prime minister of a Conservative government before World War II, offered as his symbols the bowler hat and the pipe.

Harold Wilson, the British Labour prime minister (1964–70 and 1974–1976), had been an Oxford University lecturer in economics, and with that experience he smoked at the nation without ever kindling them into flame. It was said that he needed a pipe to have something to do with his hands: they gave the impression that if he could only manage to keep his pipe alight, all his political problems could be solved.

Despite being on opposite sides of the British political spectrum from Stanely Baldwin, Labour Prime Minister Clement Attlee was also a pipe smoker—he just left off the bowler hat to give a more working-man impression.

·KING·COLE·

**Old King Cole was said to be a merry old soul, but he did not have to face the problems of Germany's ex-chancellor Helmut Kohl**

Currently another Labour politician and one of the few pipe-smoking members of the British House of Commons, Tony Wedgwood Benn, offers a sense of profound wisdom from behind a skillfully handled and expressive pipe.

Ex-chancellor Helmut Kohl of Germany was among the most impressive of European leaders to smoke a pipe. In addition to his political difficulties during 1998, he also encountered hostility from a vociferous antismoking lobby. He was shown in a cartoon published in British newspaper *The Times* as a rather sorry figure, Old King Cole, with a broken bowl and a broken pipe at his feet.

## The Smoking Detective

These attributes of the pipe smoker—contemplation, action, probity, and shrewdness—have become associated with one particular occupation, namely, the detective of fiction. Sir Arthur Conan Doyle's Sherlock Holmes with his bent pipe is the prototype. With his pipe in hand in the study he considers the case: "Watson," he said, in the story *The Red Headed League*, "It is quite a three-pipe problem."

He seems to have smoked almost anything, and, contrary to the picture generally given him, the pipe he favored in the earlier stories was a clay. After thought there is action, pipe in hand, as he embarks on the trail. Finally, he is able to offer reassurance to the innocent and an explanatory account to Dr. Watson over his evening smoke.

Georges Simenon's Inspector Jules Maigret is another pipe-smoking detective, well portrayed by Rupert Davies in the BBC television series of the

**Sherlock Holmes faces a three-pipe problem.**

# Pipe

1960s. Kindling his pipe in an ill-lit Parisian street, Maigret will be found cogitating on every aspect of the case. The facts are not enough; over his calvados at the bar, the psychology of the characters must be weighed up. Later, across the pipe rack on his office desk the suspects must be interrogated, and, after the arrest has been made, the matter has to be fully explained to his loyal team of associates at the Sureté. We feel the matter has been in safe hands. Simenon, himself, was a keen smoker.

British writer J. M. Barrie, creator of Peter Pan, tells a charming tale of amateur detection, worthy of Sherlock Holmes, in My Lady Nicotine. He describes how he hears a noise against the shared wall with his neighbor that he decides is the tapping out of a pipe. He concludes it cannot be a clay, which would break, or a meerschaum, which would be too valuable; it must therefore

**Men of the pipe: actor Rupert Davies (left) played writer Georges Simenon's (right) Inspector Maigret on British television in the 1950s and 60s. Maigret's image is synonymous with the pipe; in real life Davies was voted Pipeman of the Year in 1964.**

be a briar. Occasionally, the noise is slightly metallic, which suggests the bowl has a metal band. As this makes contact with the wall only occasionally, it suggests that the wooden rim of the pipe has burnt unevenly, probably because of a loose connection between mouthpiece and stem.

## Women and Pipes

There is no doubt that in the undeveloped world men and women smoked pipes and continue to do so where the cigarette has not replaced them. African examples have been quoted; in many places the women may cultivate the plant in a home garden while the men tend a more distant cultivation.

In the Western world there have been periods in history where feminine pipe smoking has been fashionable among the upper classes, but they rarely lasted long. Portraits can be found showing a lady holding a delicate clay, such as that of Madame Le Brun in possession of Alfred Dunhill Ltd. Most families today will probably recall an eccentric aunt who smoked a pipe, but social-

Ingres' Odalisque suggests something more than a woman relaxing on her bed. The long-stemmed pipe propped up against the right-hand wall indicates her languorousness may be due to her smoking it.

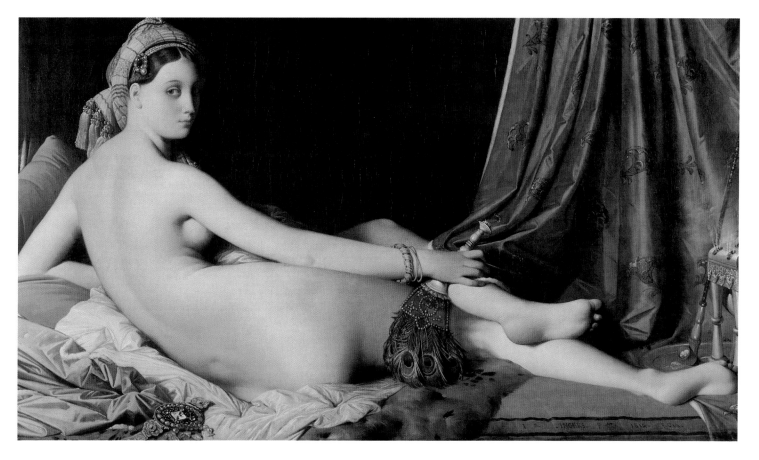

ly it has been predominantly a male habit with the women as exceptions rather than the rule.

Among manual workers, on the other hand, the habit has probably been continual from the introduction of tobacco. The clay pipe had been used steadily by many working women until the cigarette replaced it. The image comes to mind of Grandma sitting on her veranda in an Adirondack log cabin or in a Scottish

**Hippie girl lighting her pipe.**

**A turn-of-the-century Norwegian woman from Telemark smokes as she spins.**

**Above middle: A Hakka woman from Hong Kong's New Territories with her metal pipe.**

A woman from northern Thailand—while for modern women in the West, smoking a pipe is a definite statement, in Asiatic countries it is a long and continuing tradition.

Borders village. The Irish immigrants to the United States sad-dled themselves with an image that proved hard to shake off. They were seen as drunken ne'er-do-wells with butch womenfolk who smoked clay pipes—something, no doubt, to take their minds off the eternal drudgery of scrubbing floors for the wealthy.

Alas sometimes, for women, their very clothing posed a flam-mable danger, as this record of a sad instance shows:

*In 1845 there died at Buxton [in northern England] at the age of 96 a woman named Pheasy Molly who had been for many years an inveterate smoker. Her death was caused by the accidental ignition of her clothes as she was lighting her pipe at the fire.*

A few years after this incident, the British satirical magazine Punch was making fun of the "modern women" who were shown smoking, two of them cigars and one a pipe. A hundred years later it would be cigarettes.

# Pipe

# The Pipe in the Movies

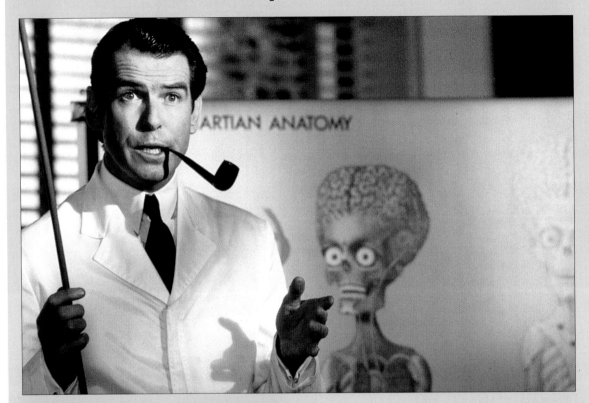

Hollywood has had a long association with the pipe; for some, smoking a pipe has been a matter of the role, for others it has been an off-screen pasttime.

Left: Pierce Brosnan recreates a Fred MacMurray role— the mad professor. In *Mars Attacks!* his pipe accentuates his eccentric Englishness.

Far left: In *Che!* Omar Sharif played the charismatic, pipe-smoking rebel with a cause, Che Guevara.

Left: Bing Crosby crooned his way through many a movie with and without a pipe. Off the screen, it was his constant companion.

It's unusual to see Charlton Heston sporting a pipe (above), but for this publicity still they probably thought it emphasized his manliness. For Edward G. Robinson (right above), the pipe adds a sinister quality, and for Gary Cooper (right) a strong, reliable, outdoors look.

# Pipe

## The Smoker Now

Under pressure from their postwar rivals—the "younger" cigarette and cigar—pipe smokers in Britain and elsewhere have set out to restore their image and bring it up to date. Since 1964 a Pipe Smoker of the Year has been nominated at an annual dinner in London given by the Pipe Smokers' Council. In 1998 the honor went to Willie-John McBride, a rugby player of distinction who has played in seventeen international tournaments for the Lions (the British Isles touring team) and sixty-three matches for Ireland. Others recognized in this way include many leading British sportsmen such as Ian Botham, the cricketer, and the former British heavyweight boxing champion Henry Cooper, as well as Sir Ranulph Fiennes, the explorer. In addition to the council other pipe clubs have been set up in Great Britain and the United States.

In a similar way, French pipe manufacturers have set out to educate their public and encourage the tradition. The Confrérie des Maîtres Pipiers of Saint Claude, which represents the makers of briars and was established in 1966, holds an annual celebration that includes the nomination of Le Premier Fumeur, or "The First Smoker of France." Their first award was in 1966 to the statesman Edgar Faure, who had been a professor at Dijon where, perhaps, he smoked at his pupils. The theme of the annual conference in 1997 was creativity, to encourage new designs of pipes in what has been a very conservative industry.

Aficionados of the venerable pipe have belied their old-fashioned image by enthusiastically embracing the opportunities afforded by that most modern of developments, the worldwide web. Here, unrestricted by borders and distance, thousands of pipe smokers can share their thoughts and opinions with their brethren in virtual companionship.

Coupled to this, the United States is seeing a resurgence of interest in pipe smoking, ironically owed in part to the boom in

The pipe smoker: we may see him as essentially a masculine figure, a doer or a thinker or both.

cigars: introduced to tobacco stores, a host of younger men have discovered the pipe and its pleasures, and deemed it worthy of a modern fashion statement.

It is tempting to try to capture the essence of the pipe smoker, to describe the characteristics that mark him out from others. We might like to distinguish him from the intolerant dictator, the hot-headed fanatic, or the overfastidious puritan and picture him as the thoughtful countryman and gardener, the inspiring professor, or the man of controlled action. We might see him as essentially a masculine figure, a doer or a thinker or both.

Yet, truth be told, in every walk of life there are those who smoke and those who do not. The habit is shared regardless of social status, occupation, race, or national origin. In an age in which the habit is not the height of fashion, those who smoke a pipe are following their own bent, and perhaps the best that can be said is that the pipe smoker is his own man. At least, if you saw a cloud of pipe smoke rising from an armchair, you would be surprised to find a woman occupying it.

Sir Compton Mackenzie, a prolific twentieth-century British author and a continual pipe smoker wrote, "I would argue that every man whatever his race, whatever his rank, whatever his profession, whatever his work is helped by smoking."

**In every walk of life there are those who smoke and those who do not; Alice meets the hookah-smoking caterpillar.**

**Men in Seattle: the United States is seeing a resurgence of interest in pipe smoking.**

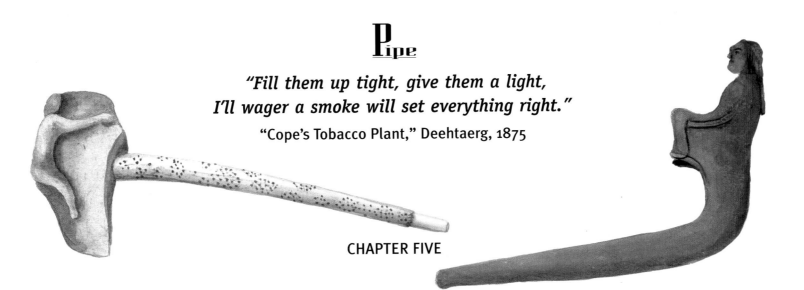

# Pipe

*"Fill them up tight, give them a light,*
*I'll wager a smoke will set everything right."*

"Cope's Tobacco Plant," Deehtaerg, 1875

CHAPTER FIVE

# Pipes Past

The problem for the pipe maker is to find a material for the bowl that will hold the smoldering tobacco safely and not become too hot to handle, and for the stem, some kind of tube that will cool the smoke and allow any noxious juices to escape before they reach the mouth. The mouthpiece must be strong enough so that the teeth do not crumble it, and the whole must enhance the flavor of the smoke and, in a civilized society, be capable of ornament.

The early Hopewell Indian culture succeeded in creating remarkable bowls from a uniformly colored porphyry. These had a slightly convex base, three to four inches long and one inch wide; the bowl, of which it formed part, was beautifully fashioned in the shape of different species of wildlife, such as birds, snakes, or animals (e.g., the beaver). One find resembled an elephant, which suggested some atavistic memory of a mammoth. These bowls were pierced at one end of the base and had no integral stem, which must have been provided by a reed or hollow stalk.

Other archæological evidence in North America includes clay pipes, and there is no reason to suppose that these were not the forerunners of the European ones.

Later pipes, by the time the Europeans arrived, were made from a soapstone that acquired the name catlinite after the nineteenth-century artist George Catlin, who painted scenes of

"A Turk smoking, sitting on a divan" by Eugène Delacroix (1798–1863), in the collection of the Louvre, Paris.

Drawings of American Indian pipes from the collection of William L. Stone: (top left) a clay pipe which resembles George Washington; (top right) clay pipe; (above) a carved slate pipe; (right) sandstone pipe made by a Tuscarora Indian.

73

# Pipe

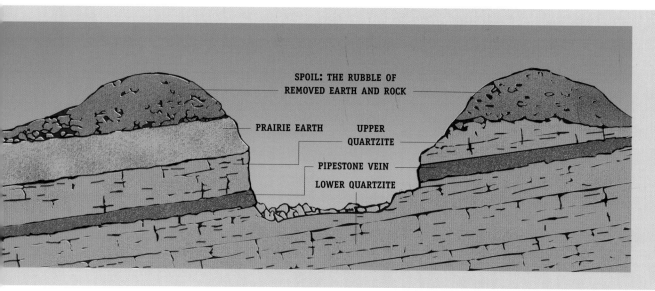

SPOIL: THE RUBBLE OF
REMOVED EARTH AND ROCK

PRAIRIE EARTH     UPPER
QUARTZITE

PIPESTONE VEIN

LOWER QUARTZITE

It takes between three to six weeks to quarry Catlinite, by digging down through the prairie earth and carefully removing the hard Sioux quartzite that sandwiches the thin seam of pipestone.

Indian life. The stone is easily worked, becoming harder on exposure to the air, and was widely traded. The largest quarry lay in Minnesota and was treated as neutral ground by different tribes to ensure safe access. This quarry is now protected as Pipestone National Monument—not to be confused with Pipe Spring National Monument in Arizona which is where a Mormon rifleman shot the bowl out of a pipe without damaging the rim!

Unlike their Hopewell forebears, the North American Indians made little attempt to sculpt their bowls, decorating instead the wooden stems with painting and carving and, as Geoffrey Turner writes in his book on the North American Indians, "finest of all, with the unbarbed guard-hair of the western porcupine." The early explorers and settlers soon encountered these pipes, which were handed around at negotiations to seal agreement—hence the famous peace pipe that the French likened to a musical reed instrument, giving it the name *chalumeau*, from which comes *calumet*.

For trading with the tribes, the Europeans speedily devised an iron-bladed tomahawk, which, with a wooden bowl on the reverse side and a hollow handle, could also be used as a pipe.

"The Indian in Washington," by George Catlin (1796–1872), shows a proud chief bearing his peace pipe, or calumet.

# Pipe

**War and peace: European traders found the combination tomahawk and pipe a useful trading implement for the North American Indian tribes.**

Plant material has often been used for the pipe making. The Russians had a long tradition of wooden pipes, and the Turks rivaled the hookah with their chibouques, which had long cherry-wood stems with red clay, flared bowls.

We have seen how the primitive smoker tried walnut shells, and in the United States, where maize or Indian corn was grown, the cob pipe became well known and can be still be found in present-day tobacconist shops.

However, wood presents difficulties: it is not normally the ideal material. For one it is combustible and the bowl burns. A thin layer of charred matter is necessary to protect the wood itself. This is why a pipe has to be "smoked in." (Modern manufacturers sometimes apply a thin layer of carbon to the new product). For another, wood is fissile—it splits; it has a variable grain according to the seasons of growth; it carries knots (which in the cheaper pipes on the market will show up as "burnouts" —holes in the side of the bowl).

## Made in England

When it proved difficult to bring the fragile Indian clay pipes home from North America, the first crude English pipes were made at the ports using West Country earth—the "little ladles" of early reports. Manufactured with improved material and techniques, the clay pipe was to be the standard instrument for smoking for the next three hundred years. Indeed, the last firm producing it closed down in the English Midlands as recently as 1989. Clay had the advantages of setting upon drying or being fired, it could form a one-piece pipe, and it could have a stem long enough to give a cool smoke.

The first models were short stemmed and small bowled, probably copying Indian originals (and also because tobacco itself was worth its weight in silver). The bowl developed with a characteristic tilt forward as if to keep the fire from the user's face, and it grew in size as the price of tobacco fell. A rectangular base was formed beneath the bowl to allow it to rest upright without

**Making clay pipes: The clay is washed in tubs (1) to remove impurities, then matured on boards (2). Air is removed from the dried clay by beating it with an iron bar (3). Clay balls are hand-rolled (4) and then formed into rough pipe shapes called "rolls."**
**(continued over...)**

1

2

3

4

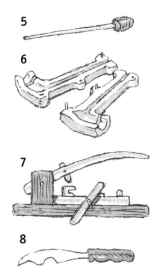

5

6

7

8

(...continued from page 75)
A piercing rod is passed through the rough shank of a roll (5) and then placed in a two-piece mold (6). The assembled mold is placed in a "Gin Press." Pulling down the lever (7) forms the hollow of the bowl, after which the piercing rod is withdrawn and the pipe removed from the mold. Dry pipes are trimmed with a knife (8), and the pipes placed in saggers (9) ready for firing to 1740° farenheit (950° c) in the kiln (10).

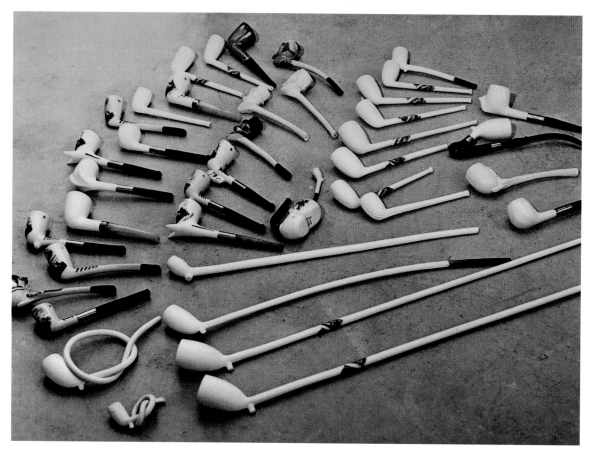

9

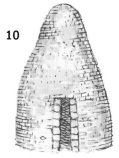

10

After firing, pipes are checked for flaws, and the mouthpiece coated with lacquer.

scorching the surface on which it sat.

Because of the astonishing speed with which the smoking habit spread, enough pipe makers were already working in Westminster to form the incorporated guild in 1619, and over a thousand of them were reckoned to be in London by 1650. They worked with metal molds, now using specialist clays from particular areas, such as Broseley in Shropshire, which also became well known for its pipes. The different manufacturers took to labeling their products with names, initials, or symbols, at first on the base then later around the bowl and, when that was decorated, on the stem. A well-known maker called Gauntlet, from Winchester, used the symbol of a glove. Of course, such labels facilitate the dating of these old pipes, which are now collectors' items, and there is a British Society for Clay Pipe Research, founded in 1983.

Discouraged by the hostility of the Stuart kings, English pipe makers took their skills to Holland and the town of Gouda, where they used clay from the river Ijssel, and developed an industry whose products dominated Europe for a hundred and fifty years.

Everywhere pipes became cheap, costing less than a farthing each (less than a quarter of an old English penny): the prudent household could order them by the gross. Inevitably their stems were fragile, and fragments are often found in old houses and yards or in riverside dumps.

Over the years the basic design changed little, but by 1750 a more sophisticated manufacturing mechanism had been developed: the gin press, which had an arm coming down vertically to punch out the bowl so that it stood at a right angle to the stem. The base diminished in size and became the characteristic spur. The mouthpiece—which posed a problem where the clay met the teeth or the wet mouth—was sometimes glazed to protect it, as in a pipe called "the Alderman."

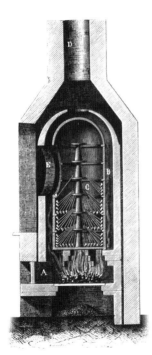

In an era of
increasing mass
production of clay
pipes, ever larger
firing kilns came
into production.

The length of the stem was important. The working man wanted something stubby and easy to handle—Jack Tar's "one of an inch," as in the verse at the start of this chapter. Short pipes, as the Scottish "cuttie" or the Irish "dudheen," were extremely popular, and it is not uncommon to find a pipe where part of the stem has been deliberately broken off to achieve the right length.

In the more leisured world of the London coffeehouses of the seventeenth and eighteenth centuries, long-stemmed pipes had become fashionable. Later, the "yard" or the "churchwarden" could be managed by Dickens's pater familias at home with his family or the Victorian cleric cheerfully composing his sermon in the vicarage study.

In competition with the meerschaum, which had begun to reach England before the Napoleonic wars, manufacturers of clays experimented with decoration. What had been confined to milling of the rim of the bowl or the marking with names became more imaginative. Queen Victoria's head can be found as a bowl, for example, or the Prince of Wales's feathers. Pipes carrying reg-

Quilp and his
friends enjoy their
churchwardens in
this "Phiz"
illustration from
Charles Dickens's
novel "The Old
Curiosity Shop."

# Pipe

78

imental crests were popular, and a common one, because it was used at masonic meetings, carries the letters R.A.O.B. and a pair of buffalo horns, for the Royal and Ancient Order of Buffaloes.

English pipe makers were not alone in their penchant for decoration, receiving plenty of rivalry from continental Europe. The French factory at Saint Omer turned out new and ever more fanciful designs: in one wonderful example the head of the Duke of Wellington forms the bowl of the pipe, with that part of the stem immediately behind him modeled on the head of a French soldier, thumbing his nose at the duke.

The clay pipe has a long and distinguished history, and it has been enjoyed by the prince and the peasant, the soldier, scholar, and working man or woman. My Scottish Borders neighbor recalls his grandmother enjoying her clay in the 1930s. She ran a small shop and, from her ropes of tobacco, sold at a halfpenny an ounce cheaper than anyone else, was able by rapid turnover to profit from the evaporation allowance (the extra weight given by the seller for the high moisture content).

**Enjoying his clay pipe, an English miner walks to work in Leeds, a basket over his arm to carry his "snap" (food and drink).**

Clay was not the only material tried; at different times silver, iron, wood, corn cobs, walnut shells, bone, glass, and porcelain were used, but each had their shortcomings. They would be too hot, too combustible, too fragile, or were not porous.

**Fanciful designs for pipe bowls were popular in the eighteenth and nineteenth centuries.**

# Pipe

In Meissen in 1750, the Germans began to make the porcelain pipes that have had a lasting effect on design. The porcelain forming the bowl and part of the stem was attractively painted, but it did not breathe—that is, allow the escape of the liquid dregs by percolation. So they designed the pipe stem to hang vertically, joined to the bowl by a Y-shaped sump at the base into which such noxious fluids could drain. The short mouthpiece and the sump were made of different materials, such as wood, horn, or amber.

The bowls of these pipes were slender, and the base, as a curious relic of the clay, often featured a small vestigial spur. Examples, perhaps now aimed at the tourist rather than the serious smoker, carry a small, perforated cap on a short chain to protect the tobacco against the weather.

**Meerschaum gave pipe craftsmen a wonderful new material from which they could carve amazingly detailed bowls.**

**Meerschaum lets a pipe smoker express himself.**

One legacy of the use of porcelain as a material has been the strong downward curve in the modern pipes known as "bents," made familiar to us through pictures of Sherlock Holmes.

British manufacturers in Staffordshire copied these European pipes, but what they produced was more for ornament than use.

## Meerschaum

Meerschaum proved a more exciting material. Originally found floating in the Black Sea, its resemblance to sea foam led to its name l'écume de mer in French and meerschaum in German. A traveler, Count Andrassy, acquired a piece of this material in Turkey and took it to a cobbler in Vienna, who made wooden pipes in his spare time. From it the cobbler made two

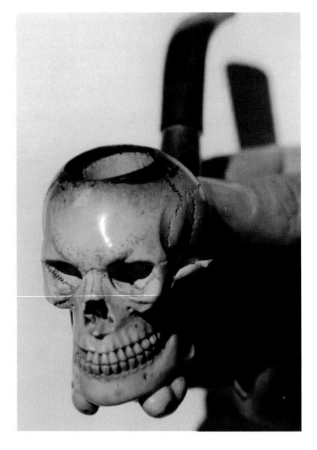

Pipe

pipes, one for the count and one for himself, and discovered that it acquired a rich brown color when he smoked it, helped by the wax on his fingers.

Meerschaum is a rare mineral of a natural gray or cream color that has the property, like catlinite, of hardening when exposed to the sun or the warmth of a room. It can be sculpted to hold fine detail, such as men with flowing beards or bolder human detail as suggested in Deehtaerg's rhyme (*see right*). To obtain its color it needs regular smoking and careful treatment. The British comedian, the late Eric Morecambe, was once seen in a Spanish hotel bringing a box into the lounge from which he unwrapped an object. As the observers watched with interest, he lit the handsome meerschaum pipe, which was, and for the whole time that he smoked it, held in a glove.

Meerschaum was originally quarried at Eski-Shehr in Turkey, where it is still worked. However, the Turkish govern-

## The Pipe in all Its Forms

*Here's to the hookah with snake of five feet*
*Or the 'portable' fix'd to one's 'topper,'*
*Here's to the meerschaum more naughty than neat*
*And here's to all pipes that are proper.*

*Here's to the Warden twelve inches of stalk,*
*Here's to Jack Tar's clay with one, sir.*
*To the pipes now with mountings so rich that they 'walk,'*
*And here's to most pipes that have none, sir.*

*Here's to the Milo just out of the shop,*
*With mouthpiece as dry as old sherry,*
*Here's to you veterans, wet as a mop,*
*Black as a sloe or a cherry.*

*Fill them up tight, give them a light,*
*I'll wager a smoke will set everything right.*

**"Cope's Tobacco Plant," Deehtaerg, 1875**

**Like Catlinite, meerschaum hardens when exposed to the air.**

81

# Pipe

ment banned further export of the raw material in 1961, so that all pipes now made from it are by Turkish craftsmen. Other sources have been found, notably in Somalia, Tanzania, and the United States, but manufacturers are naturally secretive about the origins of their material, and the rock does not seem to be of the same quality as that from Turkey.

The special qualities of the material—its lightness, its consistency, its capacity to take delicate sculpture, and especially its natural acquisition of color—gave rise to an important industry and trade for Vienna in the nineteenth century. The porous bowl absorbs the tar stains from the tobacco and holds this within a coating generally of beeswax to give the pipe its eventual golden brown color.

The Viennese realized that amber, a semiprecious material with which they were familiar, could be bored as a mouthpiece. Amber is a fossil resin to be found on the Baltic coast, and its natural yellow/light brown color added distinction to the attractive sculpture of the meerschaum bowls. The Dunhill collection contains handsome specimens of these, in particular the Marquis of Lorne's pipe, carved in commemoration of his marriage in 1871 to Princess Louise, Queen Victoria's daughter. No reputable tobacconist's window is complete without a meerschaum carrying a finely carved head and its amber mouthpiece. Both materials are now expensive, and the amber mouthpiece in modern pipes is usually replaced by one of a synthetic material.

The arrival of these ornamental pipes in the market stimulated the makers of the clays to finer designs, but the latter could never emulate the two-piece with its intricate carvings and decorated metal trimmings. Nonetheless, like the clay, meerschaum is fragile, and it remained for another chance traveler to return with the ideal material that is generally used today for the pipe bowl.

**Painting of an Austrian pipe made entirely of amber.**

**Amber had been prized for it color for hundreds of years—this is a Roman amber fruit from the first century AD—before its attractive finish and durability was recognized as ideal for making pipe mouthpieces.**

# Pipe

### Enter the Briar

The briar, not to be confused with the rose, comes from the French *bruyère*, or *Erica arborea*, a Mediterranean shrub also known as the white heath. It is said that a devotee of Napoleon went to visit the emperor's birthplace in Corsica. While there, he lost his pipe and asked a native to make him one locally. He was so impressed by what was fashioned from the briar that he took it back to France, where he encouraged the woodworkers of Saint-Claude in the Jura mountains, who already made wooden pipes, to produce it commercially.

There is more than one version of how the briar came into use since, even while Napoleon was active, the pipe makers of Cogolin in the south of France claimed to have been using its wood, which they collected from the local hillsides.

The wild Maquis of Corsica, natural habitat of *Erica arborea*, the briar from which most modern wooden pipes are made.

# Pipe

**Saint-Claude, the French capital of briar pipe manufacturing, nestles in the steep-side valley of the River Tacon in Franche-Comte, part of the Haut Jura.**

Briar grows at between 1,500 and 3,000 feet above sea level in places such as Corsica or the massifs of the French Midi. From ten to fifteen feet high, it is a plant of the Maquis, the famous woodlands where the French resistance found cover during World War II. The part of the plant that has the qualities for which it is sought is the bulbous wood at ground level between the trunk and the root. This balloonlike chunk takes thirty years to reach the right size to be worth cutting, the weight of each piece being only about seven pounds.

Briar provides a close-grained material that can be sawn, drilled, and carved and that only chars gently in the bowl. Moreover, it is light yet robust, can be decorated with silver or other trimmings, and takes a fine polish. Above all, it conveys the smoke fragrantly to the smoker's lips.

The mid-nineteenth-century craftsmen at Saint-Claude, with their long tradition of woodworking, were quick to see the advantage of such a material. A small town in the mountains at the junction of the rivers Bienne and Tacon, which originally afforded the power for the factories, became the pipe-making center of the world. It is a measure of its capacity for adjustment that, at one time producing thirty million pipes a year, its present annual production is still over seven hundred thousand. To this day Saint-Claude is the home of the leading producers of briar pipes.

Other European countries were swift to follow in French footsteps, and many of the present well-known names in the business, including Peterson of Dublin, trace their origins to this period.

For the European and North American pipe smoker, by the briar had become his chosen vessel, and it remains so today. It is treated more fully in the next chapter.

## The Corncob

The pipe made from the head of the maize or Indian corn deserves special mention. It is another uniquely North American contribution to the history of smoking. About the same time as the briar was becoming popular in Europe, an American farmer in Missouri began to make cob pipes commercially. Since then a special plant has been developed with particularly firm heads. These are then dried and cut with a saw to be shaped, drilled, and pierced to form the bowl. The bowl is strengthened in some

Light, inexpensive, cool and fragrant-smoking, but the corncob has a short life expectancy.

of the designs with plaster of paris, and a wooden base inserted. The stem, which was originally made from local reeds, is now made of sections of the cob or a synthetic material.

These handmade pipes, which are produced to different designs, remain popular and are the specialty of a firm in Washington, Missouri, with the slightly misleading name of the Missouri Meerschaum Company. The cob has the advantages of being light, cheap and providing a cool, fragrant smoke, but it also absorbs water and only has a short life. Experts recommend that the user keep one for each day of the week to make them last. Mark Twain was a great lover of the cob, and General MacArthur, as we have already seen, was its best-known patron. It is still employed by many American smokers today.

**This cat-faced pipe, made by an African tribesman from the upper reaches of the River Nile, has a bowl made from pottery, glazed brown with white markings.**

## Pipes outside Europe

Before the arrival of the modern ubiquitous cigarette, man's craving for a smoke and his ingenuity developed the pipe in the other regions of the world. The intimate relations between Brazil and West Africa based on the slave trade had introduced tobacco at an early stage to areas where the smoking of hemp was already practiced. In *The Pipe Book*, Alfred Dunhill devotes two chapters to the "Myriad Pipes of Africa." He suggests that, broadly speaking, the tribes of the savannah fashioned their pipes from clay and gourds, and those of the forests used wood.

He quotes an early description from Harris's Travels of 1607:

*[In West Africa] tobacco is to them as much as half their livelihood. And the Women are as violent Smokers as the Men...The Bowls of their Pipes are made of Clay and very large; and in the lower end of them they stick a small hollow cane, a foot and a half long, through which they draw the Smoak. And this they are not contented to have only in their mouths, but they must have it down their stomachs too, and so drink Tobacco in the strictest sense.*

**European explorers of the seventeenth century had already noted that West African women were as "violent" smokers as their men. The habit would not die with those brought to the Caribbean as slaves, and persists today, as this award-winning portrait by photographer Charles Trainor shows. Pictured is a typical banana picker on the West Indies island of St. Lucia.**

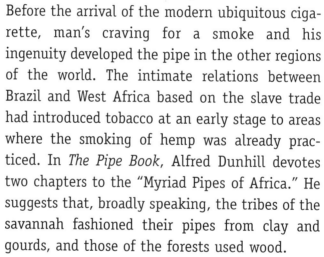

# Pipe

And from Bosman's Guinea:

*Some of them have pipes made of reeds which are about six foot long; to the end of which is fixed a stone or earthen bowl, so large that they can cram in two or three handfuls of tobacco; which pipe, thus filled, they without ceasing can easily smoke out; and they are not put to hold their pipe for being so long it rests upon the ground.*

A fine example of a pipe bowl made from a gourd.

As elsewhere, the habit spread with marvelous rapidity with all manner of materials used to form instruments for smoking. Dunhill cites the instance of a Congo tribe, the Ababua, who smoked hemp in a tube made from the midrib of a plantain leaf and tobacco from wooden pipes.

From the Cape, the Dutch influenced the design of Hottentot pipes; from the east coast, the Arabs introduced refinements to water pipes made from horn and gourds; from the Mediterranean, European and Turkish models affected the shapes of North African pipes. All manner of materials were used—pottery, stone, wood, gourds, plantains, bone, and ivory, sometimes with elaborate decoration. As often happens, the more sophisticated versions catch the collector's eye. Probably the African man or woman returning at dusk from small tobacco plots would be content with something made of clay or wood or a scroll of leaf.

Among many remarkable examples, Dunhill records King Mtesa's water pipe, made from ivory, and suggests that its design and decoration has been influenced by earlier models made from wood and gourds. The English explorer John Hanning Speke met the king in Uganda in his quest for the source of the Nile and described how he smoked his meerschaum with the dowager

**Long smoke: painting of a ten-feet-long pipe that belonged to the head of the Monbutto tribe in Zaire.**

# P<u>ipe</u>

queen while she enjoyed a pipe with a clay bowl and a long stem.

Dunhill cites another chiefly example, that of the head of the Monbutto, a tribe in Zaire. His pipe, now in the collection of the British Museum, is over ten feet long and bound from end to end with a ribbon of copper. The end resembles a leaf rib supported by two small legs.

Africa has always been a law unto itself, perhaps more influenced than influencing. Sadly, the myriad of its tribal pipes is slowly vanishing before the invasion of the ready-made cigarette. Although African pipes have had little impact on European design, there is currently a style in briars called the "calabash," which with its bold lines and a flared, slightly asymmetrical bowl resembles the shape of the African gourd.

The tribes on the coasts of northwest America beyond the Rockies probably had no contact with the tobacco cultures to the south of them. Their smoking habits and instruments depended on

**Egyptian men sit down for a sociable chat around their water pipe.**

**Egyptians, each smoking their own hookah.**

later contact with Europeans, when their indigenous skills in carving were applied to stone and driftwood to produce exotic pipes.

## The Water Pipe

The exciting pipes known as hookahs, hubblebubbles, or sheeshas, whose working has been described earlier, are still flourishing. Over centuries they developed from primitive forms—in which the water was held in a gourd, horn, or even a coconut shell—to those beautifully made from glass or pottery. The Persian kalian and the hookah have a single mouthpiece, whereas the hubblebubble has several. The water itself may be scented or even laced with alcohol and, as the device is not readily portable, it provides for a sociable as well as a cool smoke (although the Indian Moguls got around the portability problem by mounting water pipes on their elephants so that they could enjoy a smoke while out riding).

These pipes became predominant in the Islamic world, possibly because of a religious objection to allowing direct contact between tobacco and the mouth. You can still occasionally see a Muslim smoking a cigarette through his clenched fist.

The water pipe continues to be attractive to the North African hemp smoker, where it is called the "bong." A recent press report in the Emirate Times of Dubai stated that hookahs, normally served in cafés, were to be banned after midnight for moral and health reasons, which suggests they did not only contain tobacco.

**Painting of a bamboo Murut pipe from Borneo, with a stone opium bowl fixed to a Chinese-style brass bowl.**

## Asiatic Pipes

The modern traveler has to search hard for the ingenious Asiatic pipes illustrated in Alfred Dunhill's book as the advance of cigarette smoking swept away their use. The Portuguese had spread the habit of smoking in the Far East with almost greater speed than it spread in Europe, and immediately the different peoples evolved their smoking instruments with diverse local materials.

The Japanese devised metal pipes, combined with jade and lacquer, some so large that Dunhill quotes a critic of the habit giving as a reason that "there is a natural tendency to hit people over the head with one's pipe in a fit of anger."

Elsewhere pipes were made of bamboo with brass bowls and wooden mouthpieces. In the monsoon areas bamboo was of particular importance and could provide material for outsize pipes. On the other hand, Chinese pipes tended to have small bowls but were also made of bamboo, ultimately associated with the taking of opium, which did not become common practice until early in the eighteenth century. The Chinese developed their own version of the water pipe, made of metal, which could be carried easily.

**The opium habit, prevalent among the Chinese, spread to Europe as the major powers began occupying China.**

# Pipe

**Left: A Thai mother of the Meo tribe from Chiang Mai has her hands full with pipe to the front and baby to the rear.**

The Nagas of Burma also had a portable water pipe, theirs with a stone bowl above a bamboo container formed in two sections, the bottom one being detachable. The women of the tribe would enjoy a few days smoking and then pour off the much-valued foul liquid to give to their menfolk to drink, a practice occasionally found elsewhere in the world.

Siberian Eskimos acquired their smoking habits from northeast Asia but imitated the small bowls of the Asiatic tribes across the Bering Strait, who used fossilized mammoth ivory, to make pipes out of walrus ivory and decorated these with engravings of animals and hunting scenes. Dunhill describes three specimens of these as the gems in his collection.

The eastern Eskimo used a larger bowl, such as one carved from stone with a stem of wood, and a brass mouthpiece, or with a horn bowl and a bone stem.

**Above: Illustration of a walrus ivory pipe from the Bering Strait.**

**Right: A woman takes her ease, smoking the typical small-bowled Chinese pipe.**

# P̲ipe

CHAPTER SIX

# Pipes Present

Although in the United States and Western Europe the number of pipe smokers has fallen, the result has been to remove the cheaper pipes from the market and, in effect, encourage the quality production of the standard article. A visitor to any proper tobacconist will find a range of superior pipes from which to choose. He will still find some of the older ones on the shelves, such as the popular cob pipes in the United States, or the Turkish or modern meerschaums. But by far the greatest number will be briars in a great range of names and designs.

The leading center of international pipe production in the world remains at Saint Claude, where they have married the art of handicraft with the techniques of modern line production. At least forty stages can be distinguished in the production of the finished article, but the main ones can be singled out.

## The wood

*Erica arborea* grows only in the wild and must be at least thirty years old before the base of the bole is large enough for use. The collectors must search through the dense Maquis over rough ground to cut down the trunk and remove the piece required. In earlier times the first supplies were from bushes aged two hundred years or more, but now these are hard to come by.

**This handsome Barling Londoner— which costs around thirty-five dollars— with its short stem is ideal for the busy worker with little space to put it down.**

# Pipe

**The best briar still comes from Corsica.**

Originally the briar lumps came from Corsica, and then over time from other Mediterranean hillsides. Algeria became a leading producer, and thirty years of unrest there has allowed the exhausted stock to recover. Today supplies are chiefly obtained from Morocco, Spain, and Greece.

The material arrives at the factory in crude chunks that have been kept damp while in storage. Each is cut by saw into smaller pieces, boiled to remove the sap, and then dried, some, such as the best Corsican, naturally and slowly by air and some artificially.

Almost all leading pipe makers use a line system of production with machinery, but it is important to stress the role of the expert's eye at each stage to decide on the merits of the wood and grade, or even reject completely, the product. From the start, a craftsman decides the destiny of the piece in front of him. It may be suited to the rare treatment of hand carving or assigned to the three broad categories: freehand, straight, or bent.

The freehand pipe is one in which the natural grain of the wood determines the shape of the pipe, and it will

**The tools of the highly-specialized pipe-making trade, as seen at Peterson of Dublin.**

**Mid-process in the birth of a Peterson pipe: the bowl has been formed.**

**Working on the lathe is skilled precision work.**

be entirely hand worked. The straight and the bent speak for themselves: the straight is a pipe in which the bowl, stem, and mouthpiece are aligned, and the bent is one in which the stem comes from the bowl at an angle.

## The bowl and the stem.

Having been cut into smaller pieces, the wood is then crudely shaped into what will become the integral pipe bowl and stem. The bowl itself is bored, trimmed, and checked for size, and its base is rounded. Much can be done mechanically, but the curves of the pipe may have to be achieved by hand filing. The stem has to be precision drilled to provide the channel or flue into the base of the bowl, and the base of the bowl pierced to reach it. The stem has then to be further drilled to accept the tenon, sometimes called the floc, of the mouthpiece. Once again flawed material will be discovered. Knots or

A typical straight design and, below it, a bent.

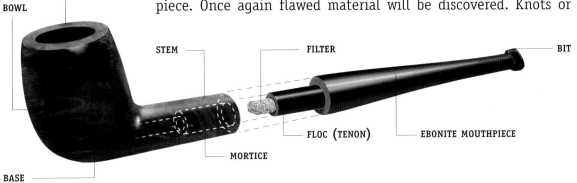

RIM
BOWL
STEM — FILTER — BIT
FLOC (TENON) — EBONITE MOUTHPIECE
MORTICE
BASE

unforeseen splits will lead to rejection. Tiny holes caused by the obstruction of growth by grains of sand, for example, can be filled with mastic and will not in themselves damage the smoking quality of the pipe.

## The mouthpiece

At one time the mouthpiece might have been of amber, bone, horn, or even part of a one-piece pipe of wood, but the modern pipe generally carries one made of vulcanized rubber (ebonite), which is strong and readily shaped. The tip of this mouthpiece, termed the bit, can also be specially shaped, more usually as a fishtail, although there are other designs.

The vulcanite mouthpiece of this Peterson pipe is checked and shaped for a perfect fit.

## Finishing

Not the least of the many processes is the finishing. The wood of bowl, stem, and the ebonite are smoothed so that they match and any signs of machining are removed. The better grade of pipes are waxed to show off their grain; others are carefully tinted before varnishing.

Many models have a metal filter, scorned by the aficionado, that is fitted between the mouthpiece and the stem so as to keep the moisture and goo out of the smoker's mouth. The final step is the important stamping with the manufacturer's name or number and the place of origin before dispatch to the market.

## The quality of a pipe

The essence of the quality of a briar pipe lies in the grain of the wood. The old wood with its dense grain is, as we have seen, rare.

**Despite modern precision tools, a human sense of touch is all important.**

**Right: From hand-spinning on the lathe to sanding and buffing, a Peterson pipe reaches completion with the careful application of silverwork (far right).**

The French rate highly the pattern of tiny circles, perhaps a cross grain, which they describe as *oeil de perdrix* (partridge eye). Other sought-after patterns are the "straight grain" with the lines running vertically from the base to the rim of the bowl, and the "flame" in which they radiate out like a fire. When they are without flaws, these grains are in the top class and increasingly costly to obtain.

# Pipe

The majority of briar pipes carry a limited number of tiny defects and are still perfectly and enjoyably smokable. In Great Britain these are rather disparagingly termed "rejects," but in the United States they are called "seconds." Their treatment in the hands of the pipe maker is not so much for concealment as it is cosmetic. The small pits can be filled with a gluey mastic mixture, or the surface can be sandblasted to scour the softer parts of the wood, which leaves a lighter and not unattractive pipe with a rougher bowl. In another finish, "rustic," the weaker parts of the bowl may be picked out by hand.

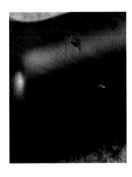

This small pit in the surface of the stem will not make the pipe unsmokable.

The surface of the bowl can be sandblasted for an attractively rough finish.

The buyer should be wary of thirds, that category of pipes with more than their fair share of flaws in which, for example, a concealed knot in the wood of the bowl may lead to a burnout and require more than cosmetic repair.

## The style of a briar

Given the nature of the wood and the selective processes of the production line, it is not difficult to see that a variety of pipes can emerge. Indeed, the pipe maker has to be aware of his discriminating market. The pattern and texture of the grain, the color and shape of the wood, together with the process of working and treating it give rise to a generous choice in the tobacconist's display case.

Following the natural lines of the grain in the briar, "freehand" or "freeform" pipes as they are sometimes called do not conform to the symmetry you expect from the standard straights and bents. In some of particular prestige, the rim of the bowl remains natural, formed from the outer wood of the tree.

## Straights and bents

The straight pipe is what most people normally think of, unless Sherlock Holmes springs to mind. It can vary in size but chiefly in the shape of the bowl, to which manufacturers, although not always in agreement, have attached names. (The straight in this

APPLE

AUTHOR

BENT

BULL MOOSE

CHUBBY

ENGLISH SADDLE

BILLIARD

CANADIAN

EGG

FOUR-SQUARE

GIANT BILLIARD

LARGE DUBLIN

context should be distinguished from the straight grain.)

The standard straight pipe with a cylindrical bowl of medium size is a "billiard"; another, for example, with a squatter bowl and a carved ring round it is called a "bulldog." Further examples can be seen on the charts to the sides of these pages. The shape of the base is important; the smoker may choose to have a rounded surface to fit comfortably in his hand or, what seems to be rare, something flat that enables the pipe to sit upright when set down.

The bent lends itself to the same variations in the bowl as well as different curves to the stem and mouthpiece. Some feel that it offers a better balance in the hand than the straight.

Straight or bent; straight grain, flame, or other; short round or deep square; waxed or varnished; sandblasted or rustic—the combinations are as many as the terms. Only the smoker himself can decide which are best suited to his profile.

## Craft by Hand and Machine

More expensive still is a pipe carved by hand. It is probably more correct to distinguish between those pipes that are made on a production line and those that are the work of one man, even though machinery will have a part in each, for example, in making the flue.

Many of the leading producers still cater for the top-quality

A finished Peterson's. Stamped in sterling silver, branded, lacquered and polished.

**OVAL BOWL**

**PEAR**

**RHODESIAN**

**SADDLE APPLE**

**SADDLE-BIT DUBLIN**

**SADDLE POT BOWL**

**LARGE POT BOWL**

**LIGHT BULLDOG**

**LIVERPOOL**

**LOVAT**

**OOM PAUL**

**PANEL**

market. Pipes may be made to personal order, perhaps with a hand-carved head, such as Winston Churchill's, for the bowl. Because such a pipe will take at least a week's labor, its price is likely to be high. Gold or silver, complete with hallmarks, may be used in bands around the end of the stem and mouthpiece or to encircle the bowl. Dunhill of London even have a pipe mounted with platinum set with diamonds!

Yet the crowning glory of the briar must lie in the grain of the wood. Pipes made from those increasingly rare pieces without defects from the older shrubs, the "firsts," which are generally kept to be worked by hand, even without embellishment, must be regarded as the princes in the pipe smoker's world.

Pipe makers may have had to turn to the production line in the face of economic reality, but they have managed to retain an art within their manufacturing. Family tradition and hand skill have been blended successfully with the use of modern machinery. At each moment, whether in the old mills of Saint Claude or the modern premises of Copenhagen, human judgment borne of experience is required. The eye and hand of the craftsman is everything.

## Production around the World

Almost all the briar pipes of the world are made within the confines of Denmark, France, Great Britain, Germany, Holland, Ireland, and Italy. Although many small specialist and reputable firms are still at work, there is only space here to describe some of the better-known makers.

Pipes from all these leading European houses and many others are obtainable in the United States, as well as painted porcelain ones from Meissen and Dresden. Most of them also produce their own blends of tobacco, catering for the discerning pipe smoker.

## France

The French have always been leading pipe makers. The briar was first used in France, and many of the leading firms were established early in the nineteenth century. It is said that Ulysse Courrieu, the founder of the House of Cogolin in the south of France, was taught by a shepherd in 1802 to make briar pipes

**SCOTCH PUG**

**SETTER**

**SLIM SADDLE APPLE**

**TOPPER**

**PRINCE**

**SADDLE-BIT BULLDOG**

**SLIM APPLE**

**SLIM BILLIARD**

from the local bushes. Today the company produces up to two hundred thousand pipes a year, half of them handmade.

In contrast, the firm of Butz-Choquin has one of the largest factories in Saint Claude, making nearly twice as many pipes on their production line as Cogolin and, in addition, providing bowls for other manufacturers. Another large-scale producer is Chacom, founded in 1825, which dries its briar naturally to ensure the quality of its pipes.

As one would expect, the French do not lag in design. Although they continue to produce classic models, they are also becoming more experimental. They have always had a tradition of hand carving carried on today by such sculptors as Paul Lanier and other specialists such as Philippe Bargiel, who works in meerschaum.

## Ireland

Peterson of Dublin is a pipe maker with an international reputation, maintaining the highest traditional standards. The company was founded in 1865 by the brothers Frederick and Heinrich Napp, who came from Nuremberg in Germany bringing their knowledge of both meerschaum and briar pipes. They set up shop in Dublin and were joined by Carl Peterson, a Latvian immigrant, who in 1894 patented the Peterson system.

Every pipe smoker knows that moisture, as well as fragments of tobacco, can collect in his pipe, and different pipe makers have supplied different answers to the problem. Peterson's solution was to design an extended stem, which drew off the smoke but then continued to a small reservoir below the bowl to gather any stray fluid.

Another innovation was a unique mouthpiece with the air hole on top so that the smoke is drawn to the roof of the mouth and less moisture escapes from it. Both these refinements can be found in Peterson's pipes today.

Peterson imports the briar in dry blocks from Morocco and Spain, prepared to its own specification, and this is then worked by hand. Add the skill of craftsmen decorating the wood with silver or gold. Peterson's silversmith, David Blake, describes his craft: "We work the silver by hand-fitting and spinning the silver on a replica of the pipe made in box wood. When it is perfect

**TAPER BULLDOG**

**WOODSTOCK**

**Above: The Butz-Choquin Rallye.**

**Right: The Peterson "Sherlock Holmes" bulldog.**

we take it off, polish it and fit it to the actual pipe, soldering it, acid cleaning it, and cleaning it and polishing it for a final time.

"I am still learning after thirty-two years in the business," he adds.

Like all pipe makers Peterson has faced a fall in demand since World War II, but it continues to produce quality, handmade pipes both from briar and meerschaum. And, as in so much of the industry, son follows father in his craft.

It is told that a tourist looking for their factory asked for directions from a Dublin police officer who looked puzzled for a moment, and then replied, "Oh, and why didn't you say so? You're looking for Captain Peterson, the man who invented smoking!"

# Pipe

## Great Britain

The name of Dunhill has become synonymous with the pipe in Great Britain. Alfred Dunhill started his business in 1893, initially providing equipment for horse-drawn carriages and then for the early automobiles. He furnished their drivers with coats, gloves, and goggles, and this interest led him to design a pipe

with a little windshield that could be smoked in the drafty, open-topped vehicles.

The sleek, simple elegance that has made Dunhill a household name.

From this unusual start he took to manufacturing his own pipes, bringing over from France an apprentice pipe maker named Joel Sasieni. Sasieni later set up his own firm, primarily exporting to the United States, where his pipes are well known.

Alfred Dunhill's philosophy, which remains the firm's, is that only the best will do, and the company uses the famous white spot to identify its classic models. These are only made with firsts—that is, the briar without flaws. It also specializes in pipes handsomely decorated with gold or silver bands that can be made to order. Like other quality pipe makers Dunhill has sub-

A classic Peterson bulldog, with trademark metalwork at the end of the stem.

sidiary companies, such as Hardcastle, producing less expensive models.

Before World War II, Dunhill had also opened shops in New York and Paris, but only the latter remains. At the London premises the company, while maintaining its marketing of high-quality pipes and tobacco, has branched out in other commercial lines in keeping with the enterprise of the founder, and the business remains a family one.

Alfred Dunhill senior was a man of many interests and had a remarkable collection of pipes from all around the world. At one time the collection was on display in the Duke Street museum. Sadly, like so many pipe collections, this one has been broken up. The newly laid out museum, however, continues to offer the visitor a display of smoking artifacts. In addition, Dunhill wrote about the history of the pipe and smoking in *The Pipe Book*, reissued by his son in 1969.

## Denmark

**A Stanwell de-luxe polished**

Proportionately, more Danes smoke pipes than in any other nation in the world. Like the Irish, a small nation, they too have their quality pipe makers— more than fifty. It was not always the case. Before World War II their pipes were imported, but when they were cut off by the conflict, they started making their own, out of beech wood or whatever was to hand.

The house of W. O. Larsen, with its shop and museum in the old part of Copenhagen, had been founded in 1864 and is now managed by the fifth generation of the family. While other pipe makers, recovering from the war, continued with traditional lines, Larsen surprised the world with a succession of freehand pipes of exciting and unusual shapes. He insisted on using the highest quality of Corsican briar that enabled him to produce top-class pipes, including those with the much sought-after bowl with bird's-eye grain.

About the same time a pipe designer of genius, Sixten Ivarsson, teamed up with Poul Nielson. Because there are a lot of Nielsons in Denmark, Poul changed his name to Stanwell. He had begun making pipes in the difficult days of the war and then set up the House of Stanwell, importing his own briar and specializing with Ivarsson in new designs. This new business was so successful that it moved to purpose-built premises in Borup in 1965. Curiously, the Danish smoker is very conservative, favoring the traditional English-style pipe, so Stanwell sells the majority of its more unusual pipes to the overseas market.

Stanwell has its own production line, selling forty-five thousand pipes a year to the

**The Charatan Grosvenor.**

home market, but for export many of the products are copies of freehand originals, retaining the characteristic idiosyncrasy. The pipes tend to have shorter bowls with flared rims, tilted back toward the smoker. Stanwell's contribution to pipe design worldwide has been important, and the pipes have found a market in the United States and elsewhere.

## Germany

The leading producer of pipes in Germany is Vauen of Nuremberg, a company founded in 1910 by the amalgamation of two older firms. It has been managed by four generations of the Eckert family and manufactures a hundred thousand pipes a year for the home market. It offers some handmade lines that use color tint-

**A fine example of German pipe maker Vauen; this jubilee creation for the Nuremberg company's 150th anniversary in 1998 was modeled after an original pipe of 1923.**

ing without hiding the grain of the wood. Vauen's distinctive mark is the white dot on the mouthpiece, which the firm claims it created before Dunhill also made it a mark of distinction.

An interesting specialist German pipe maker is Karl Heinz Joura of Bremen. As a young man in East Germany, he became a champion high-board diver before escaping from Rostock to Kiel in the days of the Berlin Wall. He trained and worked as a physical education instructor, until his hobby of pipe making proved successful enough to allow him to set up on his own. In contrast to Vauen, he makes by hand two hundred freehand pipes a year, each one unique. As the writers Liebaert and Maya say with inimitable French vividness, this adventurous background gives to his work as a pipe maker "la tenacité, l'originalite, la passion, le gout de la liberté."

## Italy

Savinelli is the best-known name for pipes in Italy. Founded in Milan in 1876 by Achille the first, it is another traditional house with a continuous family connection. Savinelli produces over three hundred thousand pipes a year chiefly for home use, but the company also makes a range of superior models with particular regard to the grain and exciting freehand models, each engraved with the signature of Achille Savinelli. They make an important contribution to the American market.

Individual Italian pipe makers have been adventurous in their designs and materials, such as experimenting with other wood (e.g., olive) and using Lucite, a translucent plastic that can be carved, for the mouthpiece.

## The United States

While the United States sends out its tobacco to the world, it has to bring back the means of enjoying it: most of its pipes or the briar with which to make them must be imported. Although the corncob pipe of Missouri is still important, and there are local traditional manufacturers of cherry-wood pipes, with their rough

A feel for the grain: many of Italian pipe-maker Savinelli's exported pipes find homes in the United States.

# Pipe

bowls, the American pipe smoker looks for the most part to Europe for the quality article.

Yet the United States has its own traditional family firms, such as the house of Peretti in Boston, which recently celebrated its 128th anniversary. Peretti offers a fine range of briar and meerschaum pipes. Although their own output is now limited, Peretti craftsmen continue to hand-carve freeform pipes using ancient Macedonian briar, where the outside surface of the tree bole can be seen forming the rim of the bowl. Peretti also blends its own tobacco mixtures and lists Bing Crosby and Basil Rathbone among its former customers.

**Basil Rathbone, seen in his famous Sherlock Holmes role, smoked Peretti tobaccos.**

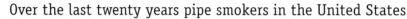

Over the last twenty years pipe smokers in the United States have taken to buying "estate" (that is, second-hand) pipes. There has always been a high value for old pipes as collectors' items but not generally for serious smoking. Today, attractive, used pipes are sought after, perhaps as an unobtainable out-of-date model, perhaps as a cheaper-than-new item, perhaps for the association with the pipe's original owner. As Richard Carleton Hacker points out in his informative *The Ultimate Pipe Book*, we do not object to putting other people's cutlery into our mouths, so why should we object to a second-hand mouthpiece, provided it has been properly disinfected?

The interested reader will find in *The Pipe Smoker's Ephemeris*, an irregular quarterly obtainable by subscription edited by the indefatigable Tom Dunn, details of a wide range of these estate pipes and of the specialist knowledge held by American aficionados. The magazine, running to some hundred pages, contains literary references, correspondence, pictures, and cartoons, and is a mine of information about pipes and tobaccos.

In particular, it provided an answer to the question about monopolistic importation of the briar: why, with the similar Mediterranean climate on its west coast, cannot the United States provide usable wood?

During World War II, when the supplies of European and North African briar were cut off, a Californian firm began to experiment with manzanita, a bearberry and member of the heath family, from which pipes were made. The wood seems to have been generally suitable, close-grained and of satisfactory smoking quality. However, it is also suggested that it was more difficult to find defect-free pieces and that the drier Californian air gave the wood a tendency to crack; or it may be that the strength of tradition favored the briar. Manzanita pipes can be found but are no longer made.

## Collectors' Pipes

As collectors' items, the trend for estate pipes in the United States has seen value in twentieth-century models (i.e., in the briars), whereas in Europe older pipes have been more sought

**A calabash with an inset meerschaum bowl .**

after. Many valuable specimens can be viewed in American museums, such as the Museum of Tobacco Art and History in Nashville, and private collections such as the Pioneers' in Colorado Springs. Private collections are occasionally broken up to release pipes onto the market.

Collectors' items include pipes of both historical interest and beautiful artistry. In the first group we should include the like of the Indian peace pipe, waved to the four winds in the sealing of an agreement, or the pipe more associated with war that Blucher is said to have flourished in triumph over the battlefield of Waterloo. William Bragge made a nineteenth-century collection of seven thousand pipes, now dispersed, which was said to have included some of Raleigh's clays. Another attributed to Sir Walter was sold at auction in 1911, described as being of wood, constructed in four pieces carrying rudely carved figures of dogs and Indians. Subsequently, it seems to have vanished.

*The Guinness Book of Records* places a meerschaum as the most valuable pipe in the world. Yet it surely has rivals in beauty. There are pipes of porcelain and glass from the German and British potteries, pipes wrought by central European metal-smiths, pipes from the wood carvers of North West America, and pipes from the east.

In 1780, a French traveler, Sonnini, describes an Egyptian pipe as being made of scented wood and some six feet long. "The most common," he says, "are wrapped in silk bound by gold wire. The part that is put in the mouth is of yellow amber, soft and sweet smelling when it is warmed or rubbed, assuaging the sharp taste of the tobacco." This is perhaps the pipe in the picture of the Seller of Pipes in a Moorish Cafe by Waldmuller.

The Germans made handsome pipes from silver in the seventeenth and eighteenth centuries, examples of which can be seen in Jacques Schmied's private museum in Lausanne, Switzerland. They would certainly be more robust than the delicately enameled and painted porcelain ones from Meissen and Dresden.

In terms of beauty it is difficult to get away from meerschaum. In addition to the Marquis of Lorne's pipe, the Dunhill collection also held a very striking one with the bowl carved into an intricate scene from the battle of Sadowa, when the Prussians beat the Austrians in 1866. The delicate combination of meerschaum and amber, even with the simpler bowls representing sculpted heads, has an immediate attraction, and they remain practical and usable. In addition to the modern conventional meerschaums sold in attractive cases for their protection, more ornate ones—whether from Turkey or elsewhere—remain available.

Pipe makers, like Larsen in Copenhagen, as well as displaying their current wares, usually hold collections from the past and thus present a history of their art to the discerning visitor.

To conclude I offer the sorry tale of my one historical, collectable pipe. I have on my desk a red curved and lined case, shaped inside to take a large meerschaum bowl and stem, a short bone mouthpiece, and a twelve-inch central stalk, also of bone. Because each part could be screwed in as required, the pipe could be smoked with or without the central section. Each junction and the rim of the bowl were mounted in initialed silver.

**Opposite page: Meerschaum pipes will always feature in collections, and The Guinness Book of Records places them as among the most valuable in the world.**

It belonged to my great-grandfather, and I have dated it by the hallmark as 1880. To my shame, I look at a half-empty case. I smoked the pipe for many years but then broke the meerschaum bowl and finally lost it while moving.

# Pipe

*"There's no sweeter tobacco comes from Virginia."*
The Virginians, William Makepeace Thackeray

CHAPTER SEVEN

# The Preparation of Pipe Tobacco

Whereas the briar is the stump of a shrub unique to Mediterranean hillsides and grows nowhere else, the tobacco plant, being tolerant of a wide range of climates, can now be found worldwide. We recognize sixty species and, after centuries of cross breeding, many thousands of varieties of tobacco, all originating from the *Nicotiana tabacum* of Central America and the *Nicotiana rustica* of the East Coast of North America.

The discovery of a trace of tobacco in an ancient Egyptian tomb some years ago surprised the academic world, until it was realized that an earlier investigator had been a heavy smoker!

The first recorded European tobacco grower was John Rolfe in Virginia, probably better known today, thanks to Disney, for his marriage to Native American princess Pocahontas. He obtained the seed of the more prolific plant from the South and grew it successfully where previously only *Nicotiana rustica* had flourished, then shipped it to England. Although tobacco has been grown in countries as far apart as Sweden and New Zealand, today's commercial crops are only

**A tobacco field in Kentucky, USA.**

**Virginian *Nicotiana tabacum*, engraved by Simeon Shaw, London 1823.**

115

found in tropical or subtropical climates, with at least 130 frost-free days.

Whatever rough, crude leaf Sir Walter Raleigh alarmed his gardener with, it must have been very different from today's sophisticated product. Modern pipe tobacco, with its breeding and planting, its mixing and blending, its cutting and shaping, and its flavoring and scenting, has a long journey before it arrives in the smoker's pouch.

## Growing and Harvesting

The chemical composition of the tobacco leaf is affected not only by highly developed processes after harvesting but also by what

it extracts from the ground during growth—a combination of the organic material and minerals. Its most important constituent is the volatile alkaloid nicotine. The plant is rapacious in its demands on the soil, and every seven years growers such as Rolfe had to carve deeper and deeper into virgin territory to clear new ground.

The American tobacco plant grows to six or seven feet high. It has large oblong leaves growing alternately on the stem and a pink flower that, if allowed to set, forms a pod containing up to a hundred thousand tiny seeds, which weigh about an ounce and are sufficient to produce enough plants for two acres. Gardeners who plant its relative, *Nicotiana alatea*, for the love-

**These young tobacco plants have just been transferred to the field.**

ly evening scent will be familiar with the small size of the seed.

The commercial plant is an annual, and each year the seedlings have to be carefully raised and transplanted. Seeds are sown in sterilized soil under screens, and the young plants are transferred to the fields when they are about six inches high. They have to be carefully protected from insects and disease; even so, Cuba once lost a large part of its crop to mildew. The soil

**The patterns of flowering *Nicotiana tabacum*.**

has to be watered if rainfall fails, and the plant kept clear of weeds and suckers.

The flowers are nipped out, as only a few are needed to provide seeds, so more growth goes into the leaves. These vary in strength at different heights of the plant, those at the base being the stronger: by stopping the stem growth at different heights, the number of leaves can be limited and their quality controlled. Harvesting may be in stages, leaf by leaf, or by cutting the whole plant, including the stem.

The nature of the plant's leaf is determined by the breeding of the seed, which is a developed science, the soil that feeds it, and the timing and manner of the harvesting.

*Nicotiana rustica* is a shorter plant with small round leaves and a yellow flower, which is usually harvested totally, stalk and leaves together. It is one of the parents of the oriental tobaccos of countries such as Turkey, and the Latakia tobacco, known by that name, grown only in Syria and Cyprus.

**A Cuban tobacco picker, with hand-cut plants, ready for drying.**

All these stages to harvesting were, and remain in many countries, labor-intensive. The historical solution in the richly soiled southern states of America and the West Indies was the plantation and slaves. While farther north in Virginia some estates used slaves, it was more common for independent farmers to struggle with family or migrant labor on smaller holdings, a practice that continues to this day despite manufacturing companies acquiring larger farms and using machines. In 1989 there were still 180,000 individual holdings in the six southern states.

## Drying and Curing

With the harvest begins the leaf's long journey from the field where it grew to the smoker who will enjoy it, which may mean crossing the Atlantic and back.

Tobacco harvesting is a labor-intensive process, even today.

The first stage is drying, a process that can be done naturally or artificially. Air curing is a natural method, where the leaf is hung in a shed for a few months to dry until it changes its color and loses its sweetness, and is used for dark tobaccos. Flue curing, an accelerated artificial process to dry the leaf within a week, is used for light tobaccos, such as Virginian, which retains its yellow color. The long process removes the sugar; the short process retains it. There are two other ways of drying tobacco. Fire cur-

Preparing lengths of leaf ready for air curing.

A tobacco barn in Boone, North Carolina, USA, packed with leaf being dried by air curing prior to shipping.

Right: Fire-curing tobacco in Malawi.

ing through the smoke of wood fires affects the tobacco's flavor, but it enabled the early growers to ship the leaves overseas and is still the method used for Latakia. The other method is sun curing, which is practiced extensively in eastern countries such as India where the climate allows it. However achieved, the drying is important in contributing to the nature and quality of the tobacco when smoked, and it removes the water, which is some four-fifths of the weight of the uncured leaf.

Some of the lighter tobaccos, such as Virginian, which has been artificially dried, or Burley, which has been allowed to dry in the air, are then simply allowed to age, when they lose their typical yellow color, and they are further heated to reduce their moisture content.

In contrast, the dark tobaccos are allowed to ferment. Like all vegetable matter in a compost heap, the packed mass of leaves heats up and alters chemically. The process must be carefully

controlled, and, in large quantities, the leaf has to be regularly turned over. As it ferments, it begins to give off its characteristic smell, which will be enjoyed by the smoker. Its nicotine content can also be moderated during the course of this treatment.

Nicotine is contained along with other gases in the smoke of the burning tobacco. It is a complex chemical, an alkaloid with similar poisonous properties to the unpleasant strychnine or the more useful quinine. The plant builds up its nicotine content as if it has no further use for the chemicals it contains. Curiously, it is also a poison. The English diarist Samuel Pepys is often quoted as giving the remains of a pipe to his cat, which killed it instantly.

Dark air- or fire-cured tobacco carries about 4 percent nicotine; the flue-cured, about 2.5 percent; and Turkish, less than 2 percent. *Tabacum rustica* has been grown to 10 percent. The manufacturers' process reduces the content, but it is the alkaloid that is alleged to be addictive. Nicotine's effect is first to stimulate the nerve endings and then to dull them. Clearly, tobacco should not be swallowed. Two or three drops on the tongue—say, fifty milligrams—could be fatal. Fortunately the smoker's intake is rarely above one milligram.

**Grading tobacco leaves ready for auction.**

**A tobacco auction in progress at an open market in Durham, North Carolina.**

## Processing and Blending

After drying and curing, producers in most countries hand over their crop to a cooperative or wholesaler. In the United States the individual grower offers his carefully graded "hands" of leaf to the manufacturer in the famous open markets.

The manufacturer accumulates a range of different tobaccos either directly or through an exporting intermediary. Color, size, maturity, and soundness must all be carefully considered by the buyer when judging and purchasing these different grades of tobacco: what the smoker will eventually savor will be a mixture of between ten and twenty grades.

There are the light tobaccos, such as Virginian, sometimes called "Bright" from its yellow color, and Burley, developed from the chance observation of an American farmer in 1869 who noticed some of his plants carried leaves with yellow streaks. There are the dark tobaccos such as Maryland, grown mostly in the state of the same name; the curious Perique, cultivated only in one small corner of Louisiana for its blending qualities; and the eastern tobaccos such as Turkish or the Syrian Latakia. Even at this point the selection of the right leaf is complex and requires skilled judgment, because each year's, each farm's, each plant's yield can vary.

A tobacco processing factory in Mexico.

Within the factory gates, tobacco is put through a series of processes, and at each stage the leaf has to be kept at the right temperature and humidity. The different grades are mixed, cut, flavored, and scented. Broadly speaking, your tobacco may be cut directly from the treated leaf, or it may be caked under intense pressure, further fermented, and then either shredded or sliced as flake in a richer blend.

A visit to one of the smaller mills in England can be illustrative and instructive. In 1792 Thomas Harrison, an enterprising young man from the small town of Kendal in the Lake District, went to the Scottish port city of Glasgow, which the "tobacco barons" had made the chief point of entry for tobacco into Great Britain. He took back from the north the knowledge of how to make pipe tobacco. Eventually, he was joined by the sensible Samuel Gawith, who had married his daughter at the black-smith's anvil in Gretna Green.

Their tobacco was transported from the coast by packhorses, and one load was so "shoogled" into powder that the firm formed the idea of making snuff as well. Waterpower was originally harnessed to drive the machines, and the snuff grinder was, until recently, the oldest piece of machinery still in commercial use in Great Britain. In the mid-nineteenth century, Samuel's two sons parted business ways, one to produce pipe tobacco and the other snuff (taking the old grinder with him).

Today, a visitor to Gawith Hoggarth's warehouse under the sign of the Turk's Head will find in miniature the process of preparing pipe tobacco. You can see the cardboard cartons of the leaf, Virginian and Burley mainly from Africa, which is cheaper than from America. Because it arrives too brittle to handle, first it has to be steamed in a six-foot bath to make it workable, so that the midribs can be removed. Preservatives must be added to prevent the leaf from rotting.

The different tobaccos are blended and the "casings" applied. These flavorings are secrets of the trade and may be anything from sugar to whisky. Normal tobaccos are made by feeding the conditioned leaf into cutting machines. Finally, the "top flavors," the romantics, are added to give whatever attractive scent is to greet the opener of the tin.

Third-generation John Gawith, who inherited the secret of these additions from his father, says, "The art of the blending is to combine different qualities and types of tobacco leaf to produce the required smoking characteristics, whether it be a very mild blend or a very strong tobacco. We must also take account of the cut of the tobacco, which affects the smoking characteristics, and the color combination to produce a blend that is pleasing to the eye. The flavors and casings are used both to enhance the natural tobacco flavors and, of course, to make an individual unique blend."

His old warehouse is a bewildering maze of rooms and stair-

**Under the sign of the Turk's Head: tobacco manufacturer Gawith Hoggarth's warehouse in Kendal, England.**

**The finished product: a selection of pipe tobaccos.**

cases. In the basement venerable cast iron machines, presses, shredders, and cutters carry out their tasks. In an upstairs room, another old machine prepares the third class of tobacco, twisting leaves into a rope. Some smokers still use this by cutting off a piece at a time and then hand-rubbing it before filling their bowl. But for a long time, this rope provided chewing tobacco for miners who were, of course, not allowed to smoke underground.

Gawith Hoggarth sends its individually prepared tobaccos to many of the three hundred tobacconists in Britain who still offer their customers the choice of mixing their own.

In contrast to the mill at Kendal stand the large-scale factories, yet the principles by which they have to operate are essentially the same. There may be more workmen, more machines, and multistoried buildings, but the process goes through the same stages to reach the same consistency and harmony of product. Premises, such as Murray's in Belfast, may keep their aromas on different floors of the building to maintain their purity, but here, too, blending has its secrets. The formula for Erinmore tobacco is said to be kept in the security of a Belfast bank.

**Blended while you wait: to suit discerning smokers, some tobacconists provided the means for clients to obtain their own taste.**

## A World of Flavors

In the end the pipe smoker is confronted by choice: the choice of color from yellow to black, reflecting the mixture of grades of leaf; the choice of cut—shreds ranging from fine (strands of 0.4 millimeters in length) to coarse (2.5 millimeters) or the flake that may come ready rubbed or curly cut; the choice of a scented product or plain, old-style "English." He has the choice of taste and how the tobacco will burn.

The so-called "American" tobaccos use a mixture of Virginian and Burley leaf with the addition of Perique and Latakia, for piquancy. Burley has particular merit as the ready absorber for the casings, and, as United States regulations allow a higher percentage of these, the tobaccos are generally moist and aromatic.

The "English" tobaccos, while using much the same mixture of leaf, are by contrast plainer and more natural, including Latakia and eastern leaf. The Dutch with their historical link to Indonesia have traditionally produced dark, strong tobaccos but, like the Danes, have moved to lighter, more aromatic ones. Both use Cavendish, which is the result of a process of double fermentation rather than a particular leaf. The Danes have in common with the British a preference for pressed tobacco, and they produce a fragrant flake.

There is a European trend, perhaps encouraged by persistent advertising during the 1960s and 70s that showed women preferring men who smoked an attractive-smelling tobacco, toward an increased use of the more aromatic, American-style tobaccos, and, indeed, much of the United States leaf crosses to Europe for blending.

The pipe smoker enjoys a great range of personal choice. Nobody would presume to nominate the best, nor would he fail to put forward his own candidate for selection. Furthermore, every pipe smoker, except in France, is able to visit any reputable tobacconist, make up his own mixture, and put that in his pipe and smoke it.

The evening sun warms maturing tobacco plants in Chiapas, Mexico.

# Pipe

*There is a real sense of pleasure in sitting before one's own fire with racks piled about, each briar, clay, or meerschaum catching the flickering light in its own way. And there is that feeling of achievement at seeing the racks, some moments later, filled with clean, sweet pipes, each ready and waiting to be filled with a favorite blend.*

Mark Twain

CHAPTER EIGHT

# The Practice of Pipe Smoking

**Ready for a puff: tobacco tins hold the key to a contented smoke.**

**P**ipes, like all good friends, need cherishing at whatever price they come. They are displayed from twenty to a thousand dollars in my local pipe shop, the latter an ornate meerschaum. My favorite briar cost twenty-five, and the tobacconist pointed out the insignificant white mark that betrays a filled-in flaw.

As stated earlier, the briar bowl requires a thin carbon lining before it smokes well. This is not true of the meerschaum or the clay but applies to all wooden pipes, which have to be broken in carefully, smoked evenly and slowly until that vital layer of carbon is formed.

# ℙipe

There are many types and blends of pipe tobaccos available, and choosing the right mix may take many months of trial and error. Although the tins in which most tobaccos are sold are a sensible way of storing the material, many pipe smokers prefer to transer it either to a pouch or a humidor. In any case, most brands will require "rubbing" to crumble the mixture before use.

For some this is a distasteful practice. My grandfather, for instance, employed his college porter to do it for him, and, I believe, once connected a basin tap to a tube with a side branch attached to his pipe stem, so that the dripping tap created the necessary draft.

One school of thought favors rubbing a thin layer of honey on the inside of the bowl before this initial smoking, and this practice is even recommended for those pipes that come from the manufacturers with a layer of carbon already in place. It has to be stressed that this layer should be kept thin—too much may overheat the pipe and crack it as well as reduce the capacity of the bowl.

The French recommend that for this breaking in the bowl should first only be partially filled and smoked with long puffs. Subsequently the amount of tobacco is gradually increased until a uniform layer of carbon lines the bowl.

# Pipe

## Lighting Up

When the pipe has been broken in, the experienced smoker may take his new friend from the rack or his pocket. He extracts his tobacco from the pouch with all the apparent wisdom of a philosopher. Then he works the strands with his fingers to ensure that they are free from lumps and carefully trickles the grains into the bowl. It is important that this first layer is lightly packed. Onto this he can gently tamp the tobacco until it is close to the rim, when another layer can be gently spread for ignition.

After rubbing the tobacco, its grains are trickled into into the bowl as a first layer, over which more tobacco is lightly tamped until it is close to the rim. Another layer is spread lightly over this for ignition.

Like pipes, matches are very much a matter of personal preference.

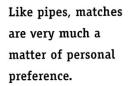

In pipe-smoking competitions, to see whose pipe on a standard fill can last longest, two matches are allowed to for lighting up. As one who goes through the household matches at an alarming rate, I can confidently say that at least two matches are required to light a full pipe. The first flame sets the top layer into smoldering curls that have to be pressed down in

# Pipe

place by the finger (preferably your own, Isaac Newton!) or with a special tamping tool (see the next section). Another flame must then be applied once more evenly across the surface of the tobacco until the first exquisite puff of smoke can be savored in the mouth and blown out.

I have already mentioned the problem

**A first flame sets the fluffy top layer smoldering. This needs tamping down before a second flame is evenly applied over the tobacco to complete the lighting up process.**

of the so-called wet smoker and solutions such as the Peterson pipe or the filter. It is not just the smoker's saliva that may accumulate: tobaccos contain their own moisture, and aromatic blends more than others. Some tobacconists sell small clay pellets that are placed in the base of the bowl to absorb this together with the tobacco tars. They only last the one fill. It is also possible to use a pipe cleaner for the same purpose, but generally the only answer when the taste becomes acrid and combustion poor is to stop and start again. As many suggest you should not smoke from a hot pipe, this may mean a return to the pipe rack.

Smoking outdoors in bad weather can be difficult and harmful. Strong wind may cause uneven burning in the bowl and damage it, sparks from it may inflict damage on clothes, and I cannot recommend going downhill on a bicycle with a thought-to-be-out pipe in one's pocket. Some pipes, such as the Tyrolean models, carry a protective metal lid.

Bear two important points in mind when knocking out the contents of the pipe. The first is to have a substantial ashtray, not one that seems likely to shatter. Sturdy stone and glass ones

130

are all right, but I prefer tapping wood on wood. The second is to hold the pipe by the bowl; do not use the stem like a hammer handle. Few tobacconists now stock new stems, and good new pipes are expensive!

**The right (above) and wrong way (opposite) to hold the pipe when knocking out the spent contents of the bowl.**

## Little Helpers

A number of useful accessories are available. The pipe cleaners that come in packets— the ones I use are very slightly tapered to enter the mouthpiece more easily—are essential unless as a countryman you collect feathers. Formerly, the tamper or stopper, shaped like a nail head and used to press the tobacco into the bowl, was often designed artistically and has now become a collector's item. Today it is more usual to find it in a bunch of little tools, the pipe smoker's

"Dibber," "tamper," or "stopper," the pipe smoker's friend is an invaluable toolkit, with a scraper, spike for the mouth stem, and a head for pressing the fill.

friend, which includes a scraper, a slender shovel for clearing the bowl, and a spike for the stem. These are sometimes embodied in the form of a penknife. I also use what I call the "hedgehog." This has a keylike handle attached to a small closed cylinder covered with short spikes that, when carefully rotated in the bowl, removes ash and excess carbon.

# ℙipe

The exterior of the bowl and stem of the briar generally keep themselves lustrous from the movements of the fingers—and some say by judicious rubbing against the nose. I have found it useful from time to time to wash out the synthetic mouthpiece. Here is one particularly pipe-saving tip. Should the synthetic floc on the mouthpiece become loose in the socket of the stem,

Pipe cleaners are vital for keeping the stem of the pipe clean.

carefully heat it and press it against a hard surface. This can succeed in expanding it that critical fraction, thereby restoring its grip.

Tobacco, too, needs its cherishing. Handsome old-style pouches (and some still in circulation) were used for its storage, which kept trickles of ash out of the pocket. Some even had a section for the pipe as well. Modern

For many who want to take up pipe smoking, an obstacle can be the lack of good advice on where to begin. The best person to ask is the specialist tobacconist who is dedicated to providing a good service to the discriminating smoker. The selection of a pipe is a personal choice, but he will advise on what type of pipe will suit the customer's smoking character—his build, face shape, hand size, and where he intends for the most part to enjoy his pipe. He will help make a choice of flavor from the many and varied ranges of tobacco. Above all he will be an enthusiast keen to induct a novice into the brotherhood of pipe smokers.

Independent specialist tobacconists can be found in all major cities and towns, and in today's modern world also on the worldwide web. The choice of shops with their own website, where you can order from the comfort of your home is substantial, and most are very well organized, as Martin McGahey's excellent tobacconist site in Exeter, England (below) demonstrates.

tobacco packaging, however, in cans and packets, is very adequate for daily use. At home there have always existed those handsome tobacco jars or humidors offering airtight accommodation, some with built-in moisturizers. These are more popular in the United States, where a full jar might represent the investment of two hundred dollars. Again, older ones have become collectors' items. It is sometimes suggested that to restore dried-out tobacco, you should put a slice of potato in your pouch. I have never found this tip to be anything but disastrous.

Pipes can be most easily stored in racks. The purist suggests that the bowls should be downward to allow drainage from the mouthpiece, but it is probably best to push a pipe cleaner into each pipe before you stow it away. Those who aspire to smoking a different pipe for each day of the week will certainly need a rack, and these tend to be functional rather than ornamental. If you are putting one on your list of birthday presents, it is best to ask to be consulted first.

**An elegant example of a desk pipe, by Comoy.**

# Pipe

*Old pipe, now battered, bruised and brown,*
*With silver spliced and linked together,*
*With hopes high up and spirits down,*
*I've puffed thee in all sorts of weather.*

"My Broken Meerschaum," C. G. Halpine, 1860

CHAPTER NINE

# The Contented Smoker

**Left: Nothing ends a Shetland Islands fisherman's day better than a quiet smoke by a blazing fire.**

**Right: Jan Cossiers's (1600–1671) painting "The Smoker" captures the pleasant moment of anticipation at lighting up.**

We must concede that smoking is an extraordinary activity. It spread from America five hundred years ago and now reaches the uttermost parts of the earth (the moon is certainly a no-go area). No other acquired habit is like it, in the sense that it preoccupies its practitioners and its enemies as with two sides of a religion.

The plant is extraordinary, unique in its acquisition of nicotine. Probably no other plant has been so well studied, so minutely tended, and so carefully prepared. For that matter, probably no other plant's sale is so subject to rules and regulation.

Although the trade in tobacco is now dominated by the giant cigarette companies, there remains, more particularly in the production of pipe tobacco, elements of personal skill, the flair of personal judgment in the grading and blending, that can be properly described as an art. The skill in the selection by feel and observation of the hands of tobacco at a North Carolina auction is a gift given to few. And the blender, whether in a large laboratory or the corner of an old mill, has to trust his nose if he wishes to retain the consistency and quality of his product.

# Pipe

The pipe, too, is the result of a discerning eye and a skilled hand, whether worked on a lathe or with a chisel. It is all the more extraordinary that the small piece at the foot of a Mediterranean shrub should form the stems and bowls for most modern pipes, crossing the Atlantic for the American devotee, while his tobacco comes back for the European.

Is there, then, an art in smoking? Those who smoke a pipe should surely complete the picture. It is after all a curious pastime, not to satisfy hunger or thirst, to hold an object in the hand to "drink tobacco." The pipe smoker is adding something to himself, not just a piece of polished wood but an item of special personal choice. That is why there is so wide a range of pipes to choose from, varying in size, shape, texture, color, balance. It is very much a matter of individual taste, a presentation of an image, as touched on earlier.

The absent-minded professor, the dedicated scientist, the wily farmer, the country policeman, the respected man of the cloth, the grandfather in his corner chair, the creative artist, the writer, do we not wish to see them all again, each inspired by his pipe?

Each also makes his own very personal selection of tobacco. How fortunate it is that with so much that is mass produced and

A balmy afternoon with a slender long-stemmed clay and a cool drop: "The peaceful drinker" by Jean Hégésippe Vetter (1820-1900).

standard in life, manufacturers, large and small, continue to produce so many blends available from the tobacconist's store. What a denial to our sense of smell if their rich aromas were to vanish from our homes and social life—the moist grandeur of the Cavendish mixture, the sweetness of the Bright Virginia, or the exotic taste of mystery in a scented Latakia.

The Elizabethan young man about town could obtain instruction on how to smoke from a London school. He was advised in 1614 to equip himself with a box to hold the tobacco (which must have been a rough lump of leaf, brought home in a sailor's bag), a pair of silver tongs to hold the glowing charcoal (preferably a kindling of juniper wood), a maple board on which to cut and shred, a ladle in case he wished to take the tobacco as snuff, a stopper to tamp down the contents of the pipe, and, of course, his clay pipe.

The present-day smoker who has not learned the art from his grandfather will find helpful the brochures of pipe makers, whether from Cogolin, Sallynoggin, or Boston.

For its smoker, the pipe is a friend and a source of pleasure. It is the symbol of the reflective man. Adam Hornbrook wrote over one hundred years ago in his novel *The Family Feud*:

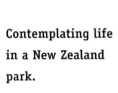

**Contemplating life in a New Zealand park.**

*What are the real evils and plagues of this age? What but its breathless fuss, its bother and din and hurry-scurry, its glare and stare and pretension. Now the pipe calms the man, lulls his restlessness, lays unruly haste and anxiety to sleep, slackens his pulse and makes a man willing to stay in his armchair and enjoy it as one of the pleasantest and most comfortable things in life, and let the world, if it will, go a-gadding.*

*Your true smoker, he that*

**A man and his pipe are a thing onto themselves...**

# Pipe

*keeps his pipe in, I mean, and that is the mark by which you may know the true from the sham smoker. He takes his time about things. You ask his opinion: the thinks twice before he answers once, keeping his pipe in. The floating upward of that light wreath of vapor often reminds him of the ethereal aspiration and play of genius or of the flight of the soul to its celestial home.*

## The Brotherhood of the Pipe

There is an another aspect of the pipe: it is the symbol of friendship. In the seventeenth century, to light a pipe at the same candle was to share a bond of friendship. In how many scenes of battle and hardship has tobacco not brought solace and a deep sense of comradeship?

The pipe-smoking fraternity embraces young and old, thinkers and doers.

# ℙipe

*Casser la pipe* (to break the pipe) for the Napoleonic soldier was to be killed in action. Not only in war but in all congenial walks of life the pipe confers a bond of fraternity on its users.

In the common room, the golf club, saloon bar, or simply on the hilltops and by the rivers, the upward curl of blue and aromatic smoke is a sign of contentment and camaraderie. The right word has to be fraternity, because, with all due respect to the ladies, the pipe belongs essentially to a man's world. J. M. Barrie's delightful book *My Lady Nicotine*, already quoted, is a happy account of life with his pipe-smoking friends, a bastion of a bachelor world before he married. On the last page he writes a poignant account of the final laying down of a cold pipe.

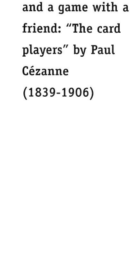

A pipe, some wine and a game with a friend: "The card players" by Paul Cézanne (1839-1906)

Our fisherman, too, is knocking out his pipe by the riverbank, carefully as his father taught him. He contemplates another cast, but the evening chill is settling. He takes down his rod, gathers together his net and the bag that had contained his lunch. After one more admiring look, he places the fish in the basket and heads for the road.

The New Inn, like all things called "new" in the right parts of America and Britain, is an old one. There is an entrance for fisherman at the back into a lobby where wet coats and waders and bags can be hung on wooden pegs, then a door into a private room. It has a low, black-beamed ceiling and walls hung with pictures of bearded, pipe-smoking anglers. High-backed chairs for the present generation are set at the table. On one side of the room is a small raised fire of logs, newly lit, and opposite hangs a set of spring scales.

The fisherman weighs his catch, enters it in the book, and takes a seat. He is soon joined by others. As the landlord brings the drinks, the men compare notes on the day in that pleasant weariness that only comes from a full stretch in the fresh air. Reverently they look at the fish and take out their pipes—well-smoked briars, a golden meerschaum, and a veteran corncob—and the anglers fill them thoughtfully.

"What," asks one, "do you reckon is the best pipe of the day?"

"The one after breakfast," says another.

"One when you've caught a fish," suggests a third.

"You wouldn't get many good smokes, then!" says the first.

Amid the laughter, the fisherman has time to complete the filling of his pipe and puts the first match to it.

"You know," he says, "I was thinking about tobacco while enjoying my afternoon pipe, and that was a very good one." He allows himself a glance at his fish. "But I don't think that we can say that anything is better after a day on the river than a smoke in good company, such as we are."

He takes another pensive puff. "I read somewhere that the motto of the first Pipe Guild in London was 'let brother love continue.' That reminded me where it all began, and I remembered Longfellow's lines from the *Song of Hiawatha*:

*"Break the red stone from this quarry,*
*Mold and make it into Peace-Pipes,*
*Take the reeds that grow beside you,*
*Deck them with your finest feathers,*
*Smoke the calumet together,*
*And as brothers live henceforward!"*

# Pipe

# Glossary

**Air curing:** the natural drying of the tobacco leaf without additional heat.

**Appalto:** the system originating in Venice whereby a government sold the monopoly of tobacco supply to a single merchant.

**Bent:** a pipe with a curved stem.

**Billiard:** a standard briar pipe with straight stem and cylindrical bowl.

**Bit, the:** the mouthpiece of a pipe which can be designed in different shapes.

**Bong:** a small, metal, North African hookah for smoking hashish.

**Briar or brier:** the white heath, *Erica arborea*, a Mediterranean shrub, the wood of which provides the bowls of most present-day pipes. Also the pipe itself. Not to be confused with the briar rose.

**Bulldog:** a style of briar pipe, with a squat, carved bowl.

**Burley:** a light tobacco used in blending on account of its natural, gentle taste and capacity for absorbing flavor.

**Burn out:** the damage caused when a knot or defect in the wood of the pipe bowl smolders to leave a hole.

**Calabash:** a gourd or pumpkin the dried, hollow shell of which can be used as a water container—such as for a primitive pipe—and may be grown to a specific shape.

**Calumet:** the Indian peace pipe from the French *chalumet*, a shepherd's musical pipe.

**Cannabis sativa:** (see also hemp) an annual, herbaceous plant, native to Asia, but now cultivated world wide, primarily for its high content of narcotic resin, both from the leaves and flowers, which can be chewed or smoked. In many countries its cultivation, possession, and use are illegal.

**Catlinite:** a red clay from the Upper Missouri region extensively used by the North American Indians to form pipe bowls; after Geo. Catlin, artist.

**Chibouque:** a long pipe smoked by the Turks.

**Churchwarden:** a clay pipe with a very long stem.

**Cob/corncob:** a pipe fashioned from the heads of specially-bred maize, chiefly in Washington, Missouri.

**Coconut:** the fruit of the coco-palm, the hard shell of which was used as a container in primitive water pipes.

**Curing:** the regulated drying of the freshly harvested tobacco leaf.

**Cuttie:** the Scots name of the short-stemmed, working man's clay pipe.

**Dudheen:** the Irishman's cuttie.

**Ebonite:** black, vulcanized rubber used for pipe stems.

**Flame:** the pattern of wood grain in a pipe bowl that radiates upward from the base.

**Floc:** (see Tenon)

**Flue curing:** the process of drying the tobacco leaf in which artificial heating is regulated by controlled drafts.

**Freehand:** the use of the natural shape of the wood to produce an idiosyncratic pipe.

**Hashish:** cannabis hemp as a drug from the derivative of which hashishin, "herb-eaters," comes our word assassin.

**Hedgehog:** author's name for a thumb-shaped implement with protruding spikes for scouring the pipe bowl to remove excess carbon, also called a "reamer."

**Hemp:** a name used for a number of plants producing fibers for rope, but also in particular for *Cannabis sativa* and its derivative drug.

**Hookah:** (see also Narghile) a pipe of eastern origin, having a long, flexible tube, the smoke being drawn through water contained in a vase.

**Hubblebubble:** a version of the preceding, perhaps with the suggestion of multiple and noisy social use.

**Kalian:** the Persian water pipe.

**Kinikinik:** a mixture of tobacco and willowbark smoked by the North American Indians.

**Latakia:** a tobacco from Syria and Cyprus, prepared by smoking the fermented leaf over a smoldering, aromatic fire, providing a powerful and rich ingredient in any blend.

**Lucite:** a translucent plastic used for pipe stems.

**Meerschaum:** a hydrous silicate of magnesium occurring in soft, white clay-like masses, originally chiefly found in Turkey, its property of setting into a porous block that could be sculpted gave rise to its use for decorated pipe bowls that turn an attractive brown after use. Hence the name of the pipe. From the German "sea foam."

**Milo:** the name of a well known Jacobean, London tobacconist and purveyor of clay pipes.

**Mortise:** (see also Tenon) the cylindrical rebate i the pipe's stem that accepts the tenon of the mouthpiece.

**Narghile:** the hookah of India, from the Persian nargil, a coconut. See items above.

**Oeil de perdrix:** literally the French meaning "partridge eye" or "bird's eye," the pattern in the grain of wood of tiny circles formed by cutting across the grain; much sought after in pipe bowls.

**Perique:** a United States tobacco cultivated in a small area of Louisiana and used to give a particular taste to blends.

**Peterson system:** an ingenious design by the Dublin firm of that name of a drainage bypass under the bowl of a pipe to draw off undesirable moisture.

**Shag:** a strong, shredded tobacco, formerly cheap.

**Sheesha:** an ornamental hookah of the Persian Gulf.

**Spleuchan:** a tobacco pouch in the Scottish Highlands, usually of leather. From the Gaelic.

**Stopper:** (see also Tamp) an implement used to tamp or stop the tobacco in the bowl.

**Straight:** a pipe with an unbent stem.

**Straight grain:** descriptive of a pipe bowl where the pattern in the wood forms parallel, vertical lines.

**Sump:** as in an engine, the rounded base of a continental, porcelain pipe in which unwanted liquid collects.

**Tamp:** the act of pressing down tobacco in a pipe bowl, particularly after the first lighting has curled it up. Can be done with the finger but less painfully with a metal tool, a tamper or stopper.

**Tenon, or floc:** the end of the mouthpiece, reduced in diameter to fit inside the mortise in the pipestem, or "shank."

**Virginian:** a widely grown tobacco, coming in different colors, mild and sweet; included in most blends.

# Bibliography

Apperson, G.L. *The Social History of Smoking*, London, Martin Secker, 1914.

ASH, (Action on Smoking and Health). *Basic Facts on Smoking*, London, 1997.

Asher, Michael, *The Last of the Bedu*, London: Viking, 1996; New York: Penguin Books U.S.A. Inc., 1996.
Ayto, Eric, *Clay Tobacco Pipes*, Princes

Risborough: Shire Publications Ltd.

Barrie, J.M. *My Lady Nicotine*, London: Hodder and Stoughton, 1890.

*Chamber's Encyclopedia.* A dictionary of universalknowledge, W&R Chambers and J.B. Lippincote Co, Philadelphia, 1895.

Corti, Count Egon, trans. Paul England, *A History of Smoking*, 1931. Reprint London, Bracken Books 1996.

Dunhill, Alfred H., *The Pipe Book*, London: A & C Black, Ltd. New York: Macmillan Co., 1924; revised edition, London: Arthur Barker Limited; New York: The Macmillan Co., 1969.

Dunhill, Alfred H., *The Gentle Art of Smoking*, London: Max Reinhardt Ltd.; New York: G.P.Putman and Sons 1954.

*Encyclopaedia Britannica*, fourteenth edition. London and New York, 1929, and fifteenth edition, 1985.

FOREST, (Freedom Organization for the

Right to Enjoy Smoking Tobacco). Audley House, Palace Street, London. Several publications: notably useful, Gabb, Sean, *Smoking and its Enemies*, 1990; Nicholson, Marjorie, *Smugglers' Charter*, 1994. Periodical, *Free Choice*.

Hacker, Richard Carleton, *The Ultimate Pipe Book*, Beverly Hills: Autumngold

Publishing, 1989. London: Andre Deutsch, 1995.

Herrman, Paul, trans. Arnold Pomerans, *The World Unveiled*, London: Hamish Hamilton, 1958.

Liebaert, Alexis, and Maya, Alain, *La Grande Histoire de la Pipe*, Paris:

Flammarion, 1993.

Nelson, David E. and others, *Pipe Smoking in the United States, 1965–1991*, Preventive Medicine 25, 1996.

Partington, Wilfred, *Smoke Rings and Roundelays*, London: John Castle, 1924.

Scott, Amoret & Christopher, *Smoking Antiques*. Princes Risborough: Shire Publications Ltd, 1996.

*Tobacco Europe*, periodical, Argus Business Media, Ltd, Redhill, Surrey.

Turner, Geoffery, *Indians of North America*, Blandford Press, Dorset. Cassell.

# Index